A GARDEN
LOST IN TIME

A GARDEN
THE MYSTERY OF THE

LOST IN TIME

ANCIENT GARDENS OF ABERGLASNEY

PENNY DAVID

FOREWORD BY PENELOPE HOBHOUSE

SPECIAL PHOTOGRAPHY BY KATHY DE WITT

WEIDENFELD & NICOLSON

CONTENTS

LEFT: *The ancient yew tunnel*

Foreword

THE GARDENS AT ABERGLASNEY in Carmarthenshire are remarkable and the story of their renewal over the last few years is gripping. The discovery and restoration of this almost vanished garden has itself been part of the process of the developing history of the site. There are still some unanswered questions. We still cannot establish a date for the original 'parapets', the feature which gives this early garden such a unique quality, although further archaeology during the 1999 season may give results. Even after five years of historical and archaeological study we still do not know whether our interpretation of the clues in the garden are accurately reflected in the 'renewed' version. In remaking the garden we can still only see it and the past through modern eyes.

Penny David's book offers a wonderfully complete picture and by interpreting the gardens and their layers of history in the context of each period she has evoked clear images of how the gardens developed through the centuries. By her diligent research she not only reflects the story of the unravelling of many of the puzzles but, steeped in knowledge of Welsh history and culture, she has evoked the true 'genius of the place'. The book is part detective story and partly a dramatic sequence of events, fortunately with a happy ending.

I first became involved in the 'idea' of Aberglasney five years ago. Then the house was a shell brooding over a bramble-covered garden, a lost demesne with only the structure of high walls and parapets, an ancient yew walk and the view to Grongar Hill to recall the ghosts. The Courtyard or Cloister Garden (as it is now named), with its broad parapets, had strong Italian overtones, pointing to a period dating to between the late sixteenth and early seventeenth century, a rare survival of a type of architectural complex which was swept away either during Civil War disorders or later when the eighteenth-century passion for the new landscape style led to destruction of earlier more structured layouts.

Gradually as the undergrowth was cleared, it became easier to understand how the rest of the garden and the walled enclosures worked around the central buildings. We could begin to recognize some of its lost characteristics. Besides the Cloister Garden and the series of walled enclosures, there was a fishpond below the Cloister Garden fed from springs which were channelled under the house, a Victorian arboretum with mid-century conifers, aviaries (or dog kennels) above the main Walled Garden, the site of an old vine house, an American garden walk leading to the church in the village and the splendid tomb of Bishop Rudd (who may have made the garden) all waiting for restoration and renewal. It was possible to imagine how orchards and kitchen gardens and more decorative flower gardens and woodland walks would have looked when the garden was first laid out, and even, with the help of Penny David's clear writing, to understand how they changed and developed through succeeding centuries.

The story of the restoration is one of dedication and, of course, surmises and discussions. From the start we had visionary leaders who formed a trust, applied for grants, found gardeners to cut the brambles and knotweed, employed archaeologists to establish dates, and experts to repair the masonry, and fired us all with enthusiasm and faith. I have been fortunate to be involved from the early stages of research and rediscovery and have had a role in redesigning one of the walled gardens.

One thing is certain; at the time of their creation the Aberglasney gardens must have been unusual. The magic and beauty of the site was still there even when all was decay and ruin. Today, with the restoration almost complete, we can recapture much of the past and look into the future. A sleeping princess has been awakened with a new public role to play. Aberglasney's future seems exciting and secure as a garden fit for the twenty-first century. Penny David has told the story of the garden's evolution and the story of the 'awakening'. She has done much of the detective work and fitted together the pieces of the jigsaw. Garden history logs a whole process and her book tells the Aberglasney story from its beginnings, to a time when the gardens were almost lost, and then goes beyond into the period of restoration. It all makes exciting reading. In a new era Aberglasney will take its place as one of Britain's most beautiful gardens, but a visit will be immensely enriched by a knowledge of its past history.

Penelope Hobhouse
Bettiscombe, April 1999

Preface

MIRACLES CAN HAPPEN. Endangered species may be rescued at the eleventh hour. Precious remnants of history are sometimes saved from ruin in the nick of time. We are on a hillside in southwest Wales. A faint piping mew makes us look upwards to see a red kite riding a thermal in leisurely arabesques. Not just one bird – a pair, a nesting pair. A few years ago these birds were almost extinct here. Now they are breeding again, and their supremely graceful aerial antics are an everyday spectacle.

Our vantage point for observing their swirling display is particularly favoured: we lean against the handsome stone of a low parapet bordering an unusual raised walkway at the core of a unique garden. A beautiful landscape stretches to the horizon around us; below, we see a series of intriguing garden enclosures inviting exploration. We are at the heart of history, but in a garden of today. We are at Aberglasney.

The Aberglasney I have come to know is very changed from the doomed, desolate place I saw on my first visit a decade ago. That was on a gloomy expedition to explore a handful of derelict or decaying gardens in the Towy valley: sobered by reading Tom Lloyd's *Lost Houses of Wales*, we shook our heads over the likely fate of these once handsome properties. Aberglasney was particularly haunting: something majestic was disappearing before our eyes – engulfed in vegetation, its fabric succumbing to gravity, greed and neglect. 'We' were a group of people from far and wide attending a meeting called 'Welsh Gardens Under Threat' and despite the apparently elegiacal tone of the proceedings I privately felt a thrill of joy. I had just come back to live in Wales, and finding such congenial activity on my doorstep was an unexpected bonus. Soon I was a member of the Welsh Historic Gardens Trust and meeting kindred spirits who enjoyed doing detective work on the forgotten gardens of our heritage.

Slowly in the next few years the destiny of some of those gardens under threat was turned around: Hafod, Dynevor and Llanerchaeron were rescued; Middleton was given an extraordinary new incarnation as the National Botanic Garden of Wales. Then I heard that things were stirring at Aberglasney – a Restoration Trust had been formed and a rescue mission on an unprecedented scale was under way – and took steps to organize a visit by our county branch of the WHGT to see what was happening.

Transformation was afoot. Where the only primary colours amid the greens and greys of ivy-clad stone had been the bright yellow dabs of dandelions and the magenta mass of willow herb, huge gaudy machines now throbbed and roared. Hard hats bobbed about, protecting the taxed brains of the Experts whose presence was required to decipher the evidence and offer solutions, and of the Artisans whose skill was to tend and mend the fabric of the garden structures – and to turn it back into a garden.

Aberglasney has always been full of perplexing mysteries, and that day we had lots of questions. What were these arches for? Who built this? What's going to happen there? How will they deal with that? Someone asked, 'Is there a book?' No; but one was needed. Suddenly I found myself appointed Storyteller, and set about trying to answer some of those questions. Aberglasney's is a detective story, a whodunnit. The myths are as tangible as the evidence. You are faced with an immense quantity of information, but a strange silence surrounds the most concrete elements of the place, a complete lack of documentation about some of its best-known occupants. Aberglasney's ghosts and legends have more reality in the common consciousness than does much verifiable fact, and they seem no less far-fetched than some of the theories put forward by scholars and experts. Actual, verifiable historical detail – someone's dates, the provenance of a particular plant, a well-recorded event – can pale beside the exploits or fate of so-and-so as firmly recorded in local memory. People who have lived in the house and on the estate tell you with some authority about the monastery that was once here; history and its sister archaeology are silent about any such establishment. Here's a ley-line, one informant will tell you; this is where the drains run, another will say. Someone will tell how they saw goats in the house, or ghosts. Rubbish! says an equally creditable witness.

The only course of action for the Storyteller is to take all these ideas – received wisdom, informed speculation, guesses, memories, associations, nuggets of knowledge, germs of fact – examine the different facets of each and try to give each its appropriate place in the fabric of a coherent story. It's a task very much like that of the stonemasons who are rebuilding and re-creating the crumbled real walls of Aberglasney's history.

It has been an unforgettable experience and a privilege for many of us (artisans, experts and recorders) to be present at the turning point. Mine has been a fascinating task – trying to capture the memories of people who have lived and worked at Aberglasney as well as the visions of those who are custodians of its future – and I suspect the task is by no means over. Readers and visitors may well know the answers to many of the queries this book has had to leave hanging in the air. And after awakening at last the Sleeping Beauty has her own life to lead, and will certainly pose her own questions.

CHAPTER ONE

Nine Green Gardens

Approaching Aberglasney:
the North Lawn and the Early Years

A PRELUDE. THE CURTAIN RISES. The scene is set. A grassy stage stretches between indeterminate massed evergreenery on either side. Our eyes are inevitably drawn to the backdrop, where the pale façade of a mansion is beginning to emerge from the gloom – severe, symmetrical, but not yet quite in focus. Is that a pillared portico adding classical grandeur to the central portion of the façade? Or is there just a raw scar of rubble etching the shallow triangle of a ghostly pediment? Some windows are open – signs of activity inside the house or of gaping dereliction? Is the stucco surface pristine, or crumbling and blurred by ivy?

And can that possibly be the glint of a chain-link fence keeping us out? As we blink a candle flame glows briefly against the dark foliage on our right, and then is gone. While some nameless Director plays these tricks with the light, the shadowy cast for the story of Aberglasney assembles on stage for a tableau. It includes lords, poets, a bishop, a boxer, lawyers, ghosts, a nabob, a teetotaller. We glimpse ladies with crinolines and croquet mallets and men with hard hats and machinery. There are bows-and-arrows, a bullet, a bomb. There are villains and heroes, tragedy and hope.

A brief preview. From the twilight of the Middle Ages emerges a line of Welsh lordlings, culminating in Sir William Thomas, whose descendants moved ever higher in status and latitude, eventually removing altogether to North Wales. For a while the families at Aberglasney fall conveniently into neat centuries. Bishop Rudd and his descendants fill the seventeenth century; the Dyers, including poet John, the eighteenth. The Phillipses or Philippses see us well into Victoria's reign, but from the 1870s the pattern fragments, and periods when the owners were in residence are interspersed by phases of letting or – as in World War Two – of troop occupation. The twentieth century has been unkind to Aberglasney, and the decades from 1960 particularly so. Human depradations and natural dilapidation brought the property to its nadir. Its future seemed hopeless until, miraculously, at the eleventh hour, a rescue operation was set in motion. Now new characters fill the stage – architects, archaeologists, experts, artisans, consultants, contractors, mingling with an audience of visitors – and a new production begins.

The story of Aberglasney spans seven (or maybe nine) centuries. It takes place in seven (or perhaps nine) separate gardens. In this book's half-dozen chapters we will make a tour of Aberglasney's gardens past and present, pausing in each one to hear a

*We glimpse ladies with crinolines and croquet mallets and men with
hard hats and machinery. There are bows-and-arrows, a bullet, a bomb.
There are villains and heroes in this tale, as well as tragedy and hope.*

chapter of the story of the people who lived and worked here, and to picture how what
we see around us might have evolved. To begin at the beginning is impossible:
Aberglasney's origins are veiled in mystery. But let us set our opening scene at the front
of the house, in what has always been the approach to Aberglasney.

The idea that Aberglasney once had nine distinct gardens, in addition to orchards and
vineyards, comes from the fifteenth-century bard Lewis Glyn Cothi, who praised the
home of Rhydderch ap Rhys, one of his many patrons, in a poem:

> *He has a proud hall, a fortress made bright by whitewash,*
> *and encompassing it all around nine green gardens.*
> *Orchard trees and crooked vines, young oaks reaching up to the sky.* [1]

Was Aberglasney, in the parish of Llangathen, that proud hall? Rhydderch ap Rhys was
the great grandson of the powerful Llywelyn Foethus (the Luxurious), Lord of
Llangathen. The family was important in medieval Carmarthenshire and held local
government posts under several kings – English ones, after Edward I's conquest of
Wales in the 1280s. The name 'Aberglasney' does not appear until later, but the place
was almost certainly the seat of this family. Apart from specific links with Llangathen,
it is unlikely for the locality[2] to have sustained more than one such sumptuous residence
with a multiplicity of gardens. The epithet 'Luxurious' only makes sense if hospitality
flowed from a hall of some splendour.

The description by the poet Lewis is one of the earliest accounts of Welsh gardens
to survive. To picture the context we must cast our minds back to the moment when
the Hundred Years War had just ended, and the Wars of the Roses were beginning; a
more peaceful timeline points us to the moment when the Gutenberg Bible was being
printed. The fact that Lewis Glyn Cothi wrote down his prolific verse has ensured its
survival. Lewis mentions only orchards, vineyards and oak woods specifically. Perhaps
these particular areas were considered important because products from each could be
a source of income – fruit and nuts, wine, and timber and bark – although we should
remember that Lewis's medium was laudatory verse rather than an estate agent's
handout or garden visitors' guide. Perhaps 'nine gardens' was a poetic flourish, and the
number merely an approximation. We shall consider this again later.

Such an affluent medieval estate would be fairly self-sufficient, with gardens providing vegetables, fruits, and herbs for culinary, household and dyeing purposes, as well as for medicinal use. There may also have been gardens surrounding a dovecote or columbarium, and gardens near fishponds, both important sources of food. A pleasure garden or 'pleasaunce' might have been situated near the private chambers of the owner, with pots and raised garden beds planted with lilies, roses, iris and peonies, with honeysuckle and other climbers possibly trained over a small trellised arbour. This garden, like the others, would have been enclosed by a stone wall, wooden paling or quickset hedge, or may have been bordered on one or more sides by a pleached double hedge that sheltered a walkway of some kind. The gardens attached to a number of fashionable gentry houses of Wales favoured long walks – so-called 'streets' in Welsh – lined with shaped trees or shrubs.[3]

It is hard to picture a garden of the Middle Ages without conjuring up colourful images derived from books of hours, altarpieces and similarly rarified sources – as if today we were to consult *Vogue* to find out what everyday life looked like. We need to translate those glowing reds and Mediterranean blues into the subtler greens and greys of the Welsh landscape. Then perhaps it becomes possible through half-closed eyes to people some of Aberglasney's enclosures with the kinsmen of Rhydderch. The half-closed eyes are necessary: perhaps some of the medieval garden divisions do coincide with the present-day ones, but the structures we see are all almost certainly later.

The name Aberglasney first seems to appear in the time of Rhydderch's grandson,

ABOVE *Looking northwards from Golden Grove across the valley of the meandering Towy. Grongar Hill (made famous by John Dyer's poem of that name) is directly opposite. Llangathen parish church sits above a pale mown field to the right of the picture. In the saddle between them, hidden still among the trees, lies Aberglasney.*

William ap Thomas (*c.* 1479–1542) – or at least, the name is retrospectively applied to his era. He was a man of great achievement, who was made a knight by Henry VIII and became the first High Sheriff of Carmarthenshire in 1541–2. He marked his success by rebuilding the chancel of Llangathen Church and adopting the fixed surname of Thomas (like many other aspiring gentry of the Tudor age, abandoning the traditional Welsh patronymic *ap*, meaning 'son of'). After this the family fortunes climbed yet higher. Sir William's son, grandson and great-grandson all married rich heiresses from leading North Wales families. They built Pen-y-bryn at Aber, a village on the coast a few miles east of Bangor, and loosened their Carmarthenshire connections. It is assumed that Aberglasney was sold in the 1590s to Anthony Rudd, Bishop of St David's. The property must have impressed the potential purchaser as a dwelling befitting the status of a bishop, or at least as an imposing home of character, ripe for improvement. We shall become better acquainted with Bishop Rudd in the next chapter. Meanwhile let's head for Aberglasney.

The place keeps its secrets well. Even its location is hard to spot from the main road between Carmarthen and Llandeilo. You can pass within five hundred yards of the house and be unaware of its existence. Nowadays this is partly because it is unwise to take your eyes off the switchback A40 and its racing traffic for an instant (in the past there would have been ruts and robbers to keep the traveller's eye from wandering). If you have leisure to look at the landscape it is the dramatic hilltops that command the skyline and the attention, not the cluster of buildings nestling into the saddle of a ridge. What reveals Aberglasney's whereabouts most plainly today is the give-away cluster of miscellaneous tall conifer shapes and misshapes standing out from the rounded profile of the deciduous woodlands and the uniform bristles of forestry plantations. You can spot the characteristic signs – the dark five-o'clock shadow of mature, or near-superannuated exotic evergreens – evidence of an old estate improved in Victorian times with vigorous conifers newly introduced.

Leave the main road at the Broad Oak crossroads and head for Llangathen. Aberglasney lies to the right, below the hill up into the village. Its presence becomes more obvious as other mature specimens, notably a handsome purple beech, proclaim the nineteenth-century owners' taste in trees. And then built structures begin to reveal themselves among the vegetation: twin classical portals flanking an entrance driveway; the house; an ancient-looking ruined tower. A cluster of service buildings becomes evident farther down the lane.

Of all Aberglasney's numerous gardens, the area through which the vistor approaches the house is hardest to define today – it lacks the physical identity of the walled enclosures and the other garden areas beyond them, and presents a miscellany of impressions: the trees, the extraordinary yew tunnel, the venerable gatehouse, and in the background, the enigmatic façade of the mansion itself. Perhaps it is the piece

of ground that has seen most metamorphosis through time as successive owners have chosen different ways of presenting a face to the world. Perhaps that is why it seems like Christmas and we have just poured a thousand-piece jigsaw labelled 'Aberglasney' on to the dining-room table. We have begun turning pieces the right way up, but many of them are still dun cardboard coloured. We can begin to sort them: sky at the top, grass down here, roof up here, architectural bits in the middle. Dark green: well, it could be yew or the evergreen trees. Or do we begin by finding all the bits with straight sides and trying to complete the frame? No, let the frame take care of itself. Let's begin by piecing together some decipherable detail that will make a focus for the rest of the picture. How about tackling what must be one of the oldest features: the gatehouse?

Gatehouse or folly? This structure has puzzled experts all through the twentieth century. The square tower, roofless, stands some three squat storeys high on our right, as we face the mansion. It seems unrelated to the other buildings – the house and the courtyard walls – to which it is set at a slightly oblique angle. A wide vaulted passage runs through it at ground level – high enough to admit a moderately laden cart, but not a man on horseback – and is decorated on the north-facing side with a moulded stone arch that does not quite belong. The building has evidently evolved. Gable-shaped projections are visible on either side of the tower to right and left about halfway up. Whereas the corners of the tower above this level are clearly defined by bulky quoins, roughly dressed and properly set, the edges of the lower part of the tower taper off into ragged stonework, suggesting that the building once continued in either direction.

ABOVE Dryslwyn Castle caps a rocky outcrop with its 'feet in Towy's flood' as poet John Dyer would say. It marks the westernmost point of the undulating ridge on which Grongar Hill, Aberglasney and Dynevor Castle sit, and also the limit of Llangathen parish.

As recently as 1990 experts declared the tower to be most probably of eighteenth-century origin, describing it as an 'C18 Picturesque folly to enhance the landscaped grounds, perhaps contemporary with the remodelling of the house by the Dyers',[4] although they acknowledged that it incorporated some medieval masonry. Given that they knew other parts of Aberglasney to have existed before that date, their thesis must have been that the building was deliberately created by someone preoccupied with the ruins of the past: the implication is that the building belongs to the time of the first two generations of the Dyer family. Such edifices were ten-a-penny in the gardens of aspiring landowners of the early 1700s, and the cleverest of them were either planned or incorporated architectural puzzles to suggest that they were the product of history and had been altered over time. A tower was a particularly esteemed type of folly, because it simultaneously fulfilled the two functions described as desirable in a garden building: 'those which are created as objects in themselves, and those from which prospects and other objects are to be viewed'.[5]

The score so far: Follies, one; Gatehouses, nil.

Then archaeologists discovered the archway to be floored with a pitched stone surface, easily capable of supporting a vehicle, and traced the remnants of walls extending to east and west. (More traces of masonry ran at right angles to the gatehouse axis alongside the yew tunnel, that most structural and substantial of vegetable creations.) It looked as if the tower was once the centre of a longer building rather like that at Corsygedol in Merioneth, which is known to date from around 1600

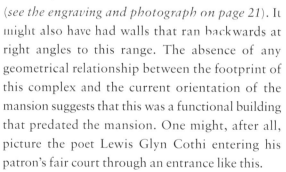

(*see the engraving and photograph on page 21*). It might also have had walls that ran backwards at right angles to this range. The absence of any geometrical relationship between the footprint of this complex and the current orientation of the mansion suggests that this was a functional building that predated the mansion. One might, after all, picture the poet Lewis Glyn Cothi entering his patron's fair court through an entrance like this.

Score in the Gatehouses vs. Follies debate: one all.

Perhaps we should call it a draw. That moulded arch has an odd quality. In itself it is probably of authentic ecclesiastical pedigree, a fragment of early architectural salvage; it simply doesn't belong in the tower at Aberglasney. When the mouldings were erected around the archway their original proportions were distorted: it looks as if the builders had to jettison at least one upright course to fit them into this low opening. The joints in the stonework

BELOW *The ruins of medieval castles stand sentinel all along the Towy valley. In its prime Dynevor was a seat of royal and princely power. From its battlements to the east we glimpse the turrets of its successor, Newton House, improved and then rebuilt by members of the Rice family during the period when the Rudds were at Aberglasney.*

are open at the back, also pointing to original construction in a taller design. Somehow this is not a very good-quality piece of follification.

When was the arch added? Any time, presumably, from the 1500s to the early 1800s, when it seems to be present in the painting with the peacock (*see pages 128–9*). It was already fashionable in the late sixteenth century to reuse old abbey fragments. The same might apply to eighteenth-century 'ecclesiasticization' of an old secular building to make it look romantic – the sort of holy dwelling a hermit might inhabit – and it was not impossible for such cosmetic adjustments to be done with an eye to possible 'sublime' effects right up to the beginning of the nineteenth century.

We may never know at what point this antique effect was cobbled on to the simple stone tower; the result was sufficiently pleasing or satisfying to subsequent generations of occupants, who retained the peculiar, useless, but intriguingly venerable building in its awkward position near the approach to the house. Rudds, Dyers, Philippses: each of the families that came from outside in successive centuries to Aberglasney were in a sense parvenus, seeking social status through acquiring land and property. While each imposed improvements of their own to bring the place up to date, none seemed prepared to sweep away completely the redundant structures of earlier periods, as so many new landowners did elsewhere. Perhaps each enjoyed the sense of borrowed antiquity and reflected pedigree, gained from living in such shadows of the past. The gatehouse became the folly in the end.

The discovery of the former extent of the gatehouse building may help to shed a glimmer of light on one of Aberglasney's most delicious enigmas, the yew tunnel or yew arch, which runs northwards from near the north-west corner of the house for perhaps thirty-odd paces. This massive growing structure exerts all the fascination and mystery that attends ancient yew trees. And nobody knows its age. This is the next part of our puzzle to work on. Endless fringes of leathery leaves of uniform deep black-green, and a cat's-cradle of trunks and branches, here solid and smoothed as waterworn red sandstone, there scaled with elongated ribbons of bark, that arch, crisscross, double back and meet and fuse together, so that in some places it is not clear at all in which direction thigh-thick branches are going or growing.

The whole tunnel at Aberglasney is composed of what looks like just five (or six or seven) huge trees, planted not quite regularly in a line that connects up with part of the now disappeared gatehouse complex and might once have paralleled a wall. Presumably they once grew vertically, but at a certain height – maybe when they reached the top of the wall that ran alongside them, or when it was dismantled – the top branches were trained over, away from the wall, until they touched the ground to make an arch high enough for a man to walk through upright. If you look carefully at the trunk side from the interior of the tunnel you can see where some branches in their flexible youth were forcibly bent over to shape the contours of the arch, and where others were drawn back

ABOVE Welsh bowmen were legendary for their prowess – think of Agincourt – and Aberglasney (or its antecedents) has several times seen arrows whistling through the air. A twelfth-century battle took place on its doorstep, and the area was again full of drama around 1400, during the rising of Owen Glendower.

parallel with the line of trunks to make its 'side'. Chunks of stone were found suspended high up in the branches of the yews in the nineteenth century, which supports the theory that a taller building once stood nearby.

When were the yews originally planted and when were they coaxed into their colossal curve? Anybody's guess. Yews are notoriously difficult to date; they grow quickly in their youth, especially in favourable conditions, but mature trees can seem to stand still and make no discernable growth for long periods of time. A free-standing, healthy yew might be dated for a couple of hundred years by conventional ring-counting. Dating yews that are growing in atypical ways – where they have been trained or topiarized, or where they are in competition in a hedge – is far more difficult. Counting of annual rings becomes fruitless. Expert Allen Meredith considered these yews at Aberglasney to be perhaps a thousand years old. Since they seem to belong to the same era as the gatehouse complex, the most conservative estimate suggests that they were planted no later than the mid-1400s. And when was the tunnel formed? To me its vaulted mass prompts distinct echoes of those other Aberglasney archways in the Cloister Garden, lying parallel a knight's-move away in the neighbouring enclosure, which we will explore in the next chapter.

It is worth noting the fact that Welsh gardeners of the late Middle Ages were as fond of clipped evergreen garden furnishings of all kinds as their English neighbours, as the vivid imagery of a number of poets testifies. Topiary was popular, but so were trees pleached and shaped to form arbours, shelters, tree houses and tunnels. By the fifteenth century 'the hedge itself had become an ornament,' to borrow from a poet's description of a Brecknock garden. 'Sometimes it was planted in a double row and so trimmed and trained that the branches became woven into a roof above. In the summer these leafy walks became green tunnels. They were called green aisles. . .'. Evidently that was a deciduous example, using something like hornbeam, but both holly and yew were also manhandled into garden buildings. A 'double hedge. . .decorated and trimmed by the shearer's skill' could make a tree house – or a tunnel. 'At its simplest it was made of holly or yew' and often sheltered a seat or bench. The Holly Carol offers an attractive picture:

*To sup wine in the middle of a hedge
In the wondrous hall of holly.*[6]

Holly and yew can be read as almost interchangeable in these descriptions: they are the two British native evergreen trees muscular and bushy enough to make such extensive garden architecture.

Although Aberglasney's tunnel of yews must have been present, and, indeed, of quite imposing size, it does not seem to have attracted comment from anyone before the nineteenth century, unless it is what John Dyer alludes to in his early eighteenth-century poem 'The Country Walk' as one of the 'gloomy bowers' of his cherished home, Aberglasney. The phrase sounds 'poetic' and loose, but could have had a specific literal inspiration. The tunnel appears first in the watercolour showing the front of the mansion in the early 1800s (*see pages 128–9*), its curved entrance echoing the archway of the gatehouse in the foreground. The greens in the painting have faded to sepia tones and it has a soft appearance, like a hedge of clipped beech holding its leaves in winter. But it is already a substantial, well-established feature. It was not sufficiently famous to lure garden-book guru and demon dendrologist John Claudius Loudon off his well-beaten track to check out more famous neighbouring properties (Dynevor, Golden

BELOW AND RIGHT *James Andrews's photograph (c. 1870) of the north lawn displays several of Aberglasney's oldest and most enigmatic features, although the yew tunnel almost obscures the grandiose portico erected on the façade by John Walters Philipps. The gatehouse tower is neatly draped in ivy. A hundred years later (right) it is surrounded by vegetation.*

The Gatehouse

LEFT *The 'inner' elevation of the gatehouse tower, facing the mansion, showing a doorway at first-floor level. To either side of the tower, gable-shaped scars at the same height indicate that the building once had single-storey extensions in each direction. Above that level the tower's corners are clearly demarcated by robust quoins, suggesting that this upper section, at least, was always a free-standing tower.*

ABOVE AND LEFT *Two period views of the arresting sixteenth-century gatehouse at Corsygedol serve as a comparison to show how Aberglasney's solitary tower might be a vestige of a longer range of buildings. Corsygedol even has a decorative moulding around the main entrance archway (as the outer face of Aberglasney's tower does), although overall the effect of its gabled roofs and dormers make it seem distractingly different.*

Grove, Middleton) in the early 1820s, when he was preparing the gazetteer section of his *Encyclopaedia of Gardening*, although he would surely have found it intriguing.

A few decades later its fame had begun to spread abroad. In their *Book of South Wales, the Wye, and the Coast*, Mr and Mrs Hall described it in about 1860 as 'a singular avenue of old yew-trees, whose stems and branches have interlaced so densely, as to form a long tunnel with living walls'. Ten years after that, photographs show the tunnel, now tightly straitlaced with Victorian severity into a low, hard curve. Its positioning curiously bears no discernable relationship to other garden features; it serves no design role in the garden plan; it is just there. It seems to be having singularly little impact on the three be-crinolined and equally restrained-looking ladies depicted on page 18 – possibly the three daughters of John Walters Philipps. In 1892 an engraving accompanied an article specifically celebrating 'the remarkable avenue or bower of trained Yews at Aberglasney' in the *Gardeners Chronicle*, this time showing a worm's-eye view of the underside of the tunnel's network of branches, and regaining some of the magic of the thing. The series of trunks emerges quite separately on the left-hand side, and some of the interweaving branch shapes depicted are quite recognizable in the tunnel of today.

As late as the 1950s Aberglasney's yew tunnel was well maintained and had a kempt look in surviving photographs, but two generations of neglect turned it into a hairy monster. Fortunately yew is renowned for its amenability to reshaping. Wildly overgrown hedges in other restored gardens have been 'stumped back' to within inches of the main trunk, only to recover in just a few years.

Whatever happens, the unique yew tunnel has become part of Aberglasney's myth, and no restoration should curb its symbolic splendour. It produces resonances that extend far beyond its unruly drama as a super-eccentric 'garden feature'. Anyone who stands in the tunnel and is irresistibly drawn to stroke the bark of its sinewy limbs feels the veneration and awe that old yews inevitably inspire. Richard Mabey calls this their 'irresistible aura of extreme antiquity'. Then there is all the associated tradition, some of it factual, much of it in the mind of the observer. Partly through their presence in churchyards, partly because of their toxicity, yews are often associated with death. They were sometimes planted over graves, especially those of plague victims, for their supposed purifying properties. It was put quite graphically at the time of Sir Rice Rudd:

> . . .because those places, being fuller of putrefaction and gross oleaginous vapours exhaled out of the graves by the setting sun, and sometimes drawn by those meteors called *ignes fatui*, divers have been frightened, supposing some dead bodies to walk, etc.[7]

That 'etc.' is a nice touch: what else might the 'dead bodies' do – turn cartwheels? Ride bicycles? And in the Aberglasney context, with its tradition of ghostly lights, that allusion to the *ignis fatuus* phenomenon – the Will-o'-the-wisp or Jack-o'-lantern – brings a pleasantly sinister *frisson*.

Other contemporaries of Sir Rice saw yew as a symbol of immortality: 'Whether the planting of yewe in Churchyards, hold not its originall from the ancient Funerall rites, or as an Embleme of Resurrection from its perpetual verdure, may almost admit conjecture.'[8] Either way, Aberglasney's yews might serve a purpose for the superstitious: the place has had its share of tragedies and hauntings. They may also have contributed to the notion that the place originated as some kind of religious settlement.

Some of the ghostly goings-on have a light-hearted air. Idris Davies who, as the gardener's young son, came to know Aberglasney's ins and outs on the eve of World War Two, reports that one of the ghosts is that of Thomas Phillips who came to Aberglasney around 1800 with a fortune from the East India Company and another man's wife. He loved the place so much that after he died in 1824 his spirit continued to haunt the grounds dressed in a frock coat and top hat. 'Never fear: it's only ol' Thomas having a look around, keeping everyone in check,' the old gardeners would say. Young Idris used to ride his bicycle through the yew tunnel, ghost or no ghost.

Yews – and the yew tunnel – are magnificent or sinister according to mood. On one visit I was exploring the tunnel, admiring the Arthur Rackham convolutions of the silky-barked branches when a small bright light caught my eye. It could have been the sun's rays penetrating a chink in the dense foliage, but the day was overcast. I went closer and breathed a sigh of relief that only slightly flustered the flame. This was no *ignis fatuus* or disembodied spirit light of the kind that we encounter in Chapter Two foretelling death. It turned out to be the steady, motionless flame of a nightlight – perched high on a level part of the branches. Who had put it there, and why? Another mystery. But it was 21 March, the spring equinox. Yews have been venerated for longer than Wales has been Christian.

The yew tunnel in its (constitutionally regulated) majesty must have been a significant presence to the generations who succeeded 'Ol' Thomas' and benefited from his legacy. We have no record of how the nephews and nieces and great-nieces of the nabob regarded the dark backdrop to their front-of-house activities. Was 'Ol' Thomas' ever 'about' to the successors of his immediate family, as he seems to have been since?

From the mid-1800s the North Lawn at Aberglasney rang episodically with the sounds of residents and visitors at the mansion enjoying the healthy outdoor pursuits that were so character-building for young people of leisure: the thud of a ball, the whistle of an arrow, the bright voices. Then there would be long periods of silence. Near the yew tunnel was the smooth, level croquet lawn. Across the lawn towards the entrance gates was the archery ground – sited in the corner of the garden nearest to the real battlefield. The raffia targets and the bows and the arrows were conveniently stored with the croquet mallets and hoops and balls in the loft above the 'hook room', next to what is now called the Gardener's Cottage; Idris Davies remembers them quietly rotting away there, disused, at the beginning of World War Two. No tennis court, oddly, although one might easily have been fitted in somewhere in the grounds of a house of the status of Aberglasney. But the motivation for creating one was absent, because no bustling family of healthy growing children was ever there.

Archery, however, was a big passion here in the 1860s, and Aberglasney's young heiress Mary Anne Emily Jane Pryse was one of its chief enthusiasts. Encouraged by Papa, Mary Anne became an expert markswoman. Soon she was shooting all over the country, taking part in events held by the Devon and Cornwall Archery Society; competing for North Cardiganshire Archers at the Annual Crystal Palace Archery Fête, and making her mark at the Irish Champion Athletic Club: 'Mrs Mayhew, whose name has often ranked high among English shooters, took second place,' the *Field* reported in 1874. By now Cupid's dart had been played. Somehow, somewhere – it is tempting to conjecture that it was through a shared interest in the sport – Mary Anne had targeted a youthful officer and become Mrs Mayhew. Shadows cloud the picture as we try to tell the story of the meeting and early married life of Major and Mrs Mayhew, later Colonel and Mrs Mayhew: they seem, as do so many Victorians, always to have been middle-aged. By the time we meet them here again around 1900 Mrs M. has been transformed into the termagant of the Temperance movement, evicting tenants who declined to sign the Pledge – but this is a turn of events we will come to later. We are at the beginning, dealing with The Early Years. There are more serious events to relate.

As these Victorian toxophilites took position in front of Aberglasney's staring façade, straight-backed, feet planted squarely, drawing their bows and aiming for the raffia bull's-eye, did any of them feel any quiver from some collective consciousness from centuries past, when arrows flew in earnest a bowshot from here, thudding not into safe raffia targets but the flesh of Norman and English invaders? The slopes of the hillside into which Aberglasney nestles once witnessed a distinctly bloody battle. It is recalled, dimly, in folk memory, with the names of the fields north of Aberglasney mansion, some of them once part of the Aberglasney demesne. But take a look at the list of Tithe dues: it tolls – no, it rings, triumphantly – with the echoes of battle as the fields north of Aberglasney are named. Cae Tranc (field of death), Cae Dial (field of vengeance), Cae yr Ochain (field of groans); the farm of Cefn Melgoed beyond Broad Oak changed its name simply to Cadfan – battlefield. The names ring rather than toll because this is Wales and it was a Welsh victory. Today's planners respect the past and do not allow bungalow-building on these fields. Over seven centuries have elapsed, and still it is remembered. How clamorously it must still have been talked of among the company in the lordly halls that our poet Lewis Glyn Cothi visited hereabouts, and how proudly it must have been remembered and rehearsed even three and a half centuries later, when Bishop Rudd first saw Llangathen.

It was Whit week, the beginning of June 1257. In England King Henry III had been having trouble with his barons; Simon de Montfort was on the scene, back from subjugating Gascony, and on the political seesaw temporarily throwing his weight on the side of Llywelyn ap Gruffydd, the last Welsh prince of Wales, and his rebellious kinfolk in the north. Early in this year Llywelyn made inroads into lordships in south-west Wales and the Gower, ravaging English settlements and shutting up the settlers in their castles. A powerful body of men under Stephanus Bauzan (Stephen Bacon), who had governed Gascony, was despatched to head inland from Carmarthen to secure the interests of the king in the Towy valley. Among their aims was to restore the English protégé Rhys Fychan to his castle and lands at Dinefwr (the modern Welsh Dynevor), near Llandeilo.

The Saxon host spent a night laying siege to Dynevor but were harassed and repulsed by skirmishing parties who knew the rocky, wooded slopes surrounding the castle. On the eve of Trinity Sunday a detachment from the main army, perhaps under Llywelyn himself, appeared from the east. The invaders decided to return towards Carmarthen along the route of the old main road. The English had formidable forces but it seems they had not scouted the tricky terrain thoroughly. The spine of undulating upland that separates the route of the main road – the Roman Via Julia Maritima, today's mundane A40 – from the River Towy runs almost due east from Llandeilo town through the rocky fastness of Dynevor and the heights of Bryn-gwrychion and Grongar (with Aberglasney saddled in between them) and on down to end in the spectacular punctuation mark of Dryslwyn Castle. On that Saturday in 1257 its woods, dingles and hidden chasms concealed hosts of Welshmen who harried the invaders mercilessly until midday. Rhys Fychan now forsook his allies and returned to Dynevor. Nevertheless 'The English, being clad in steel armour, feared nothing,' says the biased chronicler,[9] perhaps a canon still fretting years afterwards about the way Bauzan and his men had desecrated Whitland Abbey before they set out for Carmarthenshire. 'Still their mail could no more defend them than linen garments, as they placed more trust in them and their strength than they did in God.' A short distance from Llandeilo – as they drew abreast of what is now Aberglasney – they were overtaken. Near a wood called Coed Llathen they lost all their provisions, their packhorses bearing their arms and *matériel* of war, and their palfreys. Greatly encouraged, the Welsh fell upon them: they 'rushed valiantly on the mailed English, cut them down from their panoplied steeds, and in the marshes, the ditches and the dingles, trampled them beneath their horses' hoofs'.

The Battle of Coed Llathen, or Llangathen Wood, was 'the greatest battle that had ever been fought between the English and the Welsh'.[10] Three thousand dead, say the chroniclers; two thousand dead, said the histories; at least one thousand Normans or Saxons (the Welsh word for English is still *Saeson*) are estimated to have died by the most conservative reckoning.[11] The blood of the defeated Stephanus Bauzan must have run into the stream (Welsh *nant*) that drains the marshy low ground, and it gained the name Nant Stephanau. The event, in any case, would never be forgotten. The Welsh returned homewards 'laden with the spoils and arms of the enemy and a great number

RIGHT *After the 1950s no one trimmed the yew tunnel and it grew almost as high as the house. Happily, yew can take drastic pruning, and overgrown trees can be brought back into line by a programme of gradual reshaping over some years.*

BELOW *Yew seems to have a will of its own. As you look towards the house a confusion of trunks and branches vies for attention. It becomes impossible to make out and count the five, or six or seven separate original plants.*

The Yew Tunnel

ABOVE *Looking along the tunnel from the house it is evident that the original yews were planted in a line (to the left of the picture) and at some point long ago were forcibly bent over to make an arbour or tunnel. Many of the branch tips on the right have taken root and grown away themselves.*

RIGHT *Adults of average height can walk upright through the yew tunnel, but excessive trampling could damage the shallow roots. A limited access policy is planned, where children can explore the tunnel on most days, but grown-ups are allowed in only on special occasions.*

of warhorses clad in armour, and the triumph of having achieved a great victory'.

And who among the ancestry of our bard-praised acquaintance, Rhydderch ap Rhys of Llangathen, might have participated in, or witnessed, the battle? We are talking about the days of Gruffydd ab Elidir, later known as Sir Gruffydd and sometimes dubbed Knight of Rhodes, on the supposition that he earned that title on the eighth crusade of 1270–2, led by the future Edward I. Meredydd ap Rhys Grug, and his cousin Meredydd ab Owain, both chieftains of acknowledged military talent, were leading the Welsh forces. It was their nephew, Rhys Fychan, who had initially sided with the English – until he forsook them on the morning of the battle.[12] Sometime around the time of the battle of Coed Llathen, Gruffydd is supposed to have come westwards to Carmarthenshire from what is now Radnorshire to live in the lands of his wife Gwenllian's family. Since she was a descendant of the Lord Rhys, prince of South Wales, and her kinsmen were in the thick of the battle, Gruffydd ab Elidir might well have been involved too.

And what of Aberglasney? Had it been, as turn-of-the century antiquarians suggested, some kind of monastic or ecclesiastical establishment, it would no doubt have seen action. The soldiers of the approaching enemy might have stabled their horses within its walls and destroyed the altar as they had recently done at Whitland; the dying of the retreating army might have received extreme unction there. But there is no evidence of Aberglasney's existence as a religious house. Indeed, we do not know that there were any buildings there. Only the fine thirteenth-century tower of Llangathen parish church makes a recognizable landmark shared by that time and this. There is more to tell on the subject of the Welsh bowmen, including the local chaps from the neighbourhood of Catheiniog. They fight about Owen Glendower, they become famous among Henry V's archers at Agincourt, and under Henry VII they help to form the famous Beefeaters. But we stray too far.

Henry III's son, Prince Edward, succeeded his father in 1272, when he was still crusading in the Holy Land. As Edward I, the Hammer of the Scots, he hammered the Infidel and the Irish, and occasionally the Welsh as well: under him Prince Llywelyn was defeated in 1282, and two years later Wales was formally annexed to the English Crown by the Statute of Wales. It is against this background that we continue to trace the story of the ancestors of Aberglasney's early owners.

The son of Sir Gruffydd and Gwenllian was Owain. Owain ap Gruffydd is described as 'Esquire of the Body' to Edward III. Exactly how he served his king is unknown. Marrying into leading families in west Wales and holding Crown appointments was the pattern followed by the menfolk of the generations succeeding Gruffydd's arrival in the area. All the time the family was gaining in status. The place name Llangathen crops up in various family trees but is specified in the earlier mentioned poem of Lewis Glyn Cothi as the home in the early 1300s of Owain's grandson Llywelyn Foethus, Llywelyn the Luxurious. Two of his grandsons became caught up in the rising of Owen

Glendower (the Welsh Owain Glyn Dwr) against Henry IV at the end of the century, and again arrows flew through the air.

Officers of the Crown at one minute, outlaws the next, the two brothers survived their switchback course through these turbulent times. The elder brother, Rhys, held numerous increasingly prestigious posts, from Constable of two local commotes in 1386 to Sheriff of the royal county of Carmarthen in 1400. When Owen Glendower began his revolt in the next year, the younger brother Ieuan joined the insurgents, was declared an outlaw and had his lands confiscated. He fared better than his confederate Llywelyn ap Gruffydd Fychan of Caeo, described by poet Adam of Usk as 'a man of gentle birth and bountiful, who yearly consumed sixteen tuns of wine in his household'[13] but who was hanged in 1401 'with the omission of none of the customary indignities'.[14] Ieuan's lands were granted to Rhys, who remained loyal and whose fortunes continued to improve. In March 1402 the Prince of Wales granted him for life the office of Constable of Dryslwyn Castle and custody of the Royal Forest of Glyn Cothi. The next year, however – the year Harry Hotspur met his death at the Battle of Shrewsbury – Rhys switched sides; he opened the gates of Dryslwyn to Glendower on 4 July 1403. The king declared him rebel and outlaw, stripped him of his appointments and granted his lands to a Carmarthen burgess who had been despoiled. He was Thomas Dyer, who *appears* to be no relation of the family of that name who later made Aberglasney their home, although you never know.

Rhys spent several anxious years in disgrace but eventually made his peace with the king. He was pardoned in October 1409, his confiscated property was restored and he even resumed some of his royal offices – twenty five years after first holding that post, he again became Constable of Catheiniog and Maenordeilo. But these locations are still tantalizing generalities. If only we knew his actual address – the post code by which runners bearing messages in cleft sticks, or nurserymen delivering precious new plants, might have found his home.

Rhys was succeeded by his horticulturally minded son Rhydderch. 'It is certain that Rhydderch lived in the family house in Llangathen, and there can be little doubt that this was Aberglasney.'[15] It was to Rhydderch that Lewis Glyn Cothi addressed the ode that we heard about earlier. Now that we are among his contemporaries, it is time to look again at that ode and its significance for the history of our Aberglasney gardens. There must have been something special about what the bard found at Rhydderch's home. The normal gist of the traditional ode or *cywydd* is highly formulaic – rich in arcane allusions to the subject's forebears (both real and mythical) and fulsome with praise for the hospitality the bard finds at his host's hearth – obviously of fundamental concern to professional travelling poets. Although this implies an element of exaggeration, within the conventional glamorizing of the subject lie nuggets of valuable information. The flourishing career of Lewis Glyn Cothi coincided with the Wars of the Roses (1455–85), and his poetry illuminates domestic life in a way that helps to

LEFT *The mansion façade in about 1870, a generation after John Walters Philipps aggrandized it with a portico. He also made a circular sweep of drive around the front lawn, approached by a new avenue across the fields from the north west.*

complement the dry data of official records. He was on home territory here and composed odes to half-a-dozen of Rhydderch's neighbours.[16] The ode to Rhydderch stands out for its specific mention of gardens, and its particular recognition of the subject's skill at husbandry. Among the usual references to his auspicious antecedents we find one peculiarly apt comparison: there had been no one like him since Adam. Remember that 'Adam's profession' was gardening.

And what of the nine green gardens? Lewis Glyn Cothi was precise about the fact that they were all around the house. But how accurate was his counting? Were there really nine of them? Perhaps. Perhaps not. The point is that they were many, numerous, manifold – remarkably so. But here poetic conventions take over from truth. The bard is bending the language to achieve complex internal alliteration – so we cannot rely on literal meaning. And besides, he chooses to set the score at the numinous three-times-three because of its powerful mystical significance for his audience.[17] It was in *about* nine garden enclosures and orchards and paddocks close about his house – in a sort of foreshadowing of the cluster of gardens that encircle

ABOVE *The 1990s: in the triangular scar left by the pediment a circular window is revealed.*

Aberglasney mansion today – that we must picture Rhydderch seeing to the culture of his crops and the pruning of his vines and the coppicing of his oaks. A long-term project, growing oaks. The good husbandman was looking to the future.

Little is known of Rhydderch's son Thomas, and unlike his kinfolk he seems to have held no prominent positions in county affairs. No poet sang his praises in the customary ode, or at least none we know of, but perhaps his dying young prevented his

ABOVE *By the 1970s weather and neglect are taking their toll; vandalism is not far away. The wooden pediment is rotting. When it decays the free-standing columns will be easy to dismantle. Alas, the magnificent cedar of Lebanon framing this view fell in a storm of 1987.*

making his name – it did, however, earn him an elegy from our friend Lewis Glyn Cothi.[18] It was presumably in his lifetime that Henry Tudor landed at Milford Haven and made his way through Wales to Bosworth.

However, in the next generation William ap Thomas, or William Thomas (born *c.* 1479), dubbed retrospectively 'of Aberglasney' by Tudor genealogists, was back on form, making his name beyond his native Carmarthenshire by holding a succession of official appointments and contracting an ambitious marriage. His wife was Jane, the daughter of Sir William Herbert of Coldbrook in Monmouthshire and granddaughter of Sir William Griffith, Chamberlain of Gwynedd and the richest and most powerful man in north-west Wales.[19] In our Aberglasney story the link forged by this marriage is particularly significant. In establishing close relations with North Wales, our family began the process by which it would eventually quit Carmarthenshire completely, leaving the stage represented by their Llangathen properties empty for a new set of players to make an entrance as a new century began.

The union of Sir William Thomas and Jane Herbert was successful by all accounts in another sense: the couple had seventeen children, a healthy quorum of whom survived and had issue. (No wonder Sir William's will specified a bequest of his plate to 'the Lady my bedfellow'.) In Sir William Thomas, 'Knight Banneret of Aberglasney', we at last have an almost three-dimensional character emerging out of the murky past to be dimly illuminated by our footlights. He was more or less a contemporary of Henry VIII's, whom he served. As one of the more eminent figures among our Aberglasney owners, he deserves some attention. Aside from the milieu into which he was brought by his well-connected in-laws, Sir William's career was exemplary and extended far beyond the confines of Carmarthenshire. It began with his appointment as Groom of the Chamber in the household of Prince Arthur, whose wedding he attended. He also served Prince Henry (later Henry VIII) and attended his wedding and coronation. His close involvement with the royal household qualified him to testify about the marital status of both Prince Arthur and Prince Henry in 1529. He saw military service in the French expedition of 1513, the year in which he was knighted. Much of his life was spent in Shropshire and London. He was regularly Justice of the Peace in the border counties and sat on commissions concerned with the administration of South Wales, the Marches and the border shires. He was well rewarded for his services and acquired honours, grants of public office and land. Amongst other widely dispersed properties in Wales and the Welsh Marches he leased the newly dissolved Carmarthen priory on 20 May 1537.[20] It is interesting to note this tenuous ecclesiastical connection with Aberglasney, two generations or more before Bishop Rudd came on the scene. For how long did the lease last, we wonder?

Interesting, too, that towards the end of his life his activities brought him firmly back to his home territory. He had held the post of Constable of Carmarthen Castle in 1509; he became the first High Sheriff of the newly constituted Carmarthenshire in 1541–2. He survived for only a matter of months after serving in this role. He asked to be buried in the 'new chancel' of the church at Llangathen. The pull of home was strong and Sir William chose to be laid to rest there. The fact that his will was proved in London, not locally, is additional testament to the high profile of himself and his family.[21]

The son and heir of Sir William and Lady Jane was Rhys Thomas (called Rice William in his father's will), dubbed in pedigrees as 'of Aber, co. Carnarvon ; ancestor of the Coed Helen family'. Although he obviously kept a toehold in Carmarthenshire, serving as its High Sheriff in 1565, that description by genealogists shows the magnetic draw of the north and he held office there too.[22] His wife Jane was the daughter of Sir John Puleston of Caernarfon and the widow of Edward Griffith of Penrhyn. Once again it was a good match, bringing auspicious North Wales connections. The Thomases are said to have 'moved from Carmarthenshire to Aber about the middle of the 16th century'.[23]

Their son was the second of the three William Thomases in the last four generations that bring our original Welsh line of Aberglasney owners to a close. He is distinctly 'memorable' in the *1066 And All That* sense for his glorious death in 1586 commanding a force of two hundred Welshmen under the Earl of Leicester against the Spanish at the battle of Zutphen. (His even more memorable brother-officer Sir Philip Sidney was mortally wounded in the same battle.) Captain William Thomas had kept the family connection with Carmarthenshire, serving as High Sheriff in 1576 and in 1582; apparently, 'Aberglasney remained his chief residence'[24] although it is difficult to see how he could have fitted in much residing there with all his other commitments. His marriage further tightened his ties with the north, where he chalked up yet more High Sheriffdoms and MPships for the family records.[25]

When Captain William Thomas died at the age of thirty-five his son (the very last of our own William Thomases – although we shall encounter another man of that name) remained a ward of the Queen until he came of age. He inherited the lordship of Aber, which was granted as a reward for his father's bravery at Zutphen. He is described as owning estates in Carmarthenshire and North Wales and held the usual catalogue of county offices. However, we are at last released from the geneological detail; we do not even need to know what advantageous marriage he made, and who his mother-in-law was descended from. Sir William Thomas (1572–1633) lived and remained in Caernarfon. He had become what Welsh speakers around Aberglasney might (rather disparagingly) call a '*Gog*' – a North Walian. He finally loosened his hold on the family's Carmarthenshire estates. We do not know the exact circumstances, but sometime between 1594 and 1614 – and probably in the earlier part of that period – Bishop Rudd acquired a considerable proportion of those estates. Presumably he bought them from that Sir William Thomas.

As we move towards our next chapter and the Cloister Garden, where we will further ponder what the Bishop might have found to build on when he arrived, we find ourselves back near the mansion with one last major portion of the front-garden jigsaw to complete. It is the big question of Who Pinched the Portico? Who Pilfered the Pillars? Quite a substantial structure to sneak out under your coat. Not your routine job for the light-fingered.

For a hundred and fifty years Aberglasney's façade was graced by a classical portico with eight Ionic columns. It seems to have been added to the house early in Queen Victoria's reign, probably around the time when its upwardly mobile owner John Walters Philipps became High Sheriff of Carmarthenshire in 1841. He carried out a number of improvements that made the approach to the property more imposing, as befitted the home of a public figure of some standing; visitors would be impressed as they drove along the new avenue he had cut across the fields from the main road, remnants of which still stand. The portico was certainly in place in the 1860s, and forms the backdrop to the ladies in crinolines photographed in around 1870.

It disappeared in the years when Aberglasney's fortunes were perhaps at their lowest ebb. Since flooding and neglect early in the century, the state of parts of the house had gone from bad to worse. In the late 1980s the mansion was subjected to wild see-sawing swings of attention – valiant attempts at repair at one moment, vandalism and theft at the next. The columns disappeared in May 1992 and the theft was reported to the local borough council. By September the council was told that a report was being prepared with a view to prosecution. The pillars had turned up.

They had also turned up in print. Andrew Threipland, one of the loose band of people who were watching Aberglasney's fate with some concern, was browsing through a Christie's catalogue when a mention of Aberglasney caught his eye. A set of eight columns was included in the catalogue for Christie's sale of 'Garden Statuary, Architectural fittings and Chimneypieces' at Wrotham Park, Hertfordshire, on Tuesday 25 May 1993 at twelve noon. A photograph in the catalogue showed four from the set of eight, standing in line against a woodland backdrop. Item 74 was stated to be:

> A SET OF EIGHT STONE COLUMNS, each with an Ionic capital, the column formed from six tapering sections, with a stepped stone base (one capital replaced, damaged), 19th century.

The measurements were given; the provenance was stated as 'ABERGLASNEY, Llangathen, Wales', and the expected price was set at £8000–12,000. A descriptive note alluded to the source of the design: 'The noble Ionic capitals of this elegant Grecian colonnade, are inspired by the Propylaea, the entrance doorway to the Athenian Acropolis, and derive from an engraving in James Stuart and Nicholas Revett's, *Antiquities of Athens*, 1762.' The catalogue entry specified that the columns were to be dismantled and removed from Wrotham Park 'at the purchaser's expense, by appointment with Christie's'.

At the sale an unsuspecting buyer paid £17,000 for the columns. However, Christie's was alerted of the circumstances within the 28-day settlement period, and before the buyer had 'dismantled and removed' the pillars and taken possession of his spoil. There was 'a long legal battle' in the words of the *Western Mail*, but eventually the columns were returned to 'a secret location' in Wales. On 11 November 1993, magistrates at Llandovery found one Malcolm Miller (whose partner Maggie Perry owned Aberglasney) guilty under Sections 7 and 9 of the Planning (Listed Buildings and Conservation Areas) Act 1990 of doing unauthorized work to a listed building. On 8 December that year he was sentenced to 140 hours' community service. We will meet Malcolm Miller again in Chapter Six.

The case of the pinched portico held a special accidental bonus for students of Aberglasney. It was already well known that the first of the Dyers to live here had undertaken an ambitious modernization of the entrance front bringing the house into line with contemporary fashion. Dyer refaced the front in the Baroque style of the day with three storeys, equal in height, of tall camber-headed windows and inserted a round window over a now-vanished but perhaps once elaborate door frame. This round window is clearly visible in the triangular imprint left by the missing pediment. Ever since the Victorian portico had been erected it had remained hidden, along with traces of the lime mortar which coated the stone in a warm honey-tones of umber. Its uncovering reveals the sheer high quality of the early Georgian or perhaps Queen Anne architecture in the tradition that was just being evolved by James Gibbs and Nicholas Hawksmoor. There must indeed have been an elaborate door frame to underpin this punctuation mark. If only a sketch of his home by John Dyer would turn up!

The excellence of the hidden proportions also reveals one of the dilemmas facing restoration projects. To which of a building's successive incarnations do the restorers revert? The twentieth century (and the Commissioners of Ancient Monuments) have become somewhat more attached to Aberglasney's portico than the portico has been attached to the house to which it belongs! Thus it was Listed, thus it must be. If the columns had slipped their moorings earlier, perhaps, and restoration enthusiasts had come upon the scene later, we might well all have been happy to restore Robert Dyer's beautiful façade.

To accommodate the portico the two pairs of windows on either side of the central doorway and the outer pairs of the central five second-storey windows were modified into pairs of taller ground-floor windows that would fill the space below the pediment. The ghostly shapes of the original windows were also visible once the pediment was taken away. Behind the portico, inside the house, various simultaneous Victorian 'improvements' took place in the grand entrance hall two storeys high with its ornate plasterwork, and fine stained glass inserted over the staircase. It is a measure of the timelessness of classicism that in both forms, with portico and without, Aberglasney's façade is handsome.

The fiasco of the disappearing portico bore extraordinary fruit for Aberglasney in an entirely different way: besides contributing intellectually to our architectural knowledge it proved to be the very practical turning point in Aberglasney's fortunes. The story added a *frisson* of melodrama to a talk on 'The Great Gardens of Wales: Their Loss and Rediscovery' that William Powell Wilkins, founder and chairman of the Welsh Historic Gardens Trust, gave to a small but select audience of Garden Conservancy members at the National Arts Club in New York City in November 1993. The programme note said that Mr Wilkins would highlight the work of the Trust in identifying and preserving the distinguished gardens of Wales – many of them little known. One of them, of course, was Aberglasney. One particular member of that audience was smitten by the story of the derelict house behind the portico, and even more by the sad state of its gardens. He took the speaker out to dinner to hear more. Soon he was taking a plane across the Atlantic to see for himself, and eventually the Anonymous Donor was taking out his cheque book. Aberglasney was working its spells once again. The spells worked both ways: that initial cheque primed the pump for the copious amounts of funding and effort that acquiring and transforming Aberglasney and its gardens would need. The Aberglasney Restoration Trust was under way.

CHAPTER TWO

Too Much Arithmetic

The Riddle of the Cloisters and
the Coming of the Rudds

BRIGHT PAPER LANTERNS decorate the yew tunnel and the garden walls. Light floods from the windows of the house. Dance music is in the air, mingled with bright voices, laughter, whispers. There is canoodling in the cloisters – the mysterious 'monks' cells' are just right for explorations of all kinds. The war is over; the Evanses are having a party and a new crowd of young cousins and friends are at their first dance, many making their first visit to the strange old house with its legends and hauntings, its mouldering garden buildings, buried treasure and a Bishop's bath. Aberglasney has come to life again.

For a few brief years around 1950 the Cloister Garden, which is our setting for this chapter, hummed with activity: parties and balls and entertainments. The Battle of Solferino was enacted here as part of a pageant (just as long ago bullets flew here in earnest). Then tragedy hit the Evans family and they sold up and left. Blankets of brambles and knotweed hid an enigma already disguised in Victorian times beneath layers of earth and artifice. The bright young things of the party are grandparents now, only their lively memories lighting up that period of the past. And it is the archaeologists meanwhile who enlighten as they trench and sift and discover what lies further, deeper, beneath the surface.

A moment's orientation. Leave the front façade around the corner of the house nearest the yew tunnel and you are in a slightly sloping broad rectangle of garden. Stand with your back to the house looking downhill, towards the southwest and Grongar Hill, and you are hemmed in on three sides by massive ranges of stonework, variously pierced and penetrated with archways. These are no run-of-the-mill walled-garden walls, a couple of courses thick and studded with vine-eyes for the training of fruit trees. Aberglasney's courtyard walling has the bulk of fortifications. This is serious stonework. Along the top between low parapets runs a path the width of a small country road. In clear weather this elevated 'prospect walk' lures you upwards to explore – to enjoy the prospect – but on a dull day the stones have a lowering, sullen mood and the dark arches scowl unfathomably.

The Cloister Garden has lain at the heart of Aberglasney's enigma. No one knows who made it. It is unique: there is nowhere else quite like it – yet people find in it echoes of other places, either gardens they have visited, or ones read about in books, glimpsed in drawings or described by travellers. Today's visitors to Aberglasney are as captivated

'It requires but little effort on the part of a wanderer in this charming garden of old times to people the place once more with the gentlemen and pretty ladies of Jacobean times.'

and mystified by this enigmatic garden as their many predecessors have been.

In this arena we find drama in the clashing of rival theories. For decades, and all through the 1990s, it has been a duelling ground between ranks of historians, archaeologists and experts, all with different ideas about the Cloister Garden (or courtyard garden or sunken garden or prospect garden) – they don't even agree on what to call it.[1] If it is early, and classically inspired, why the crudity and lack of strict symmetry? If it is late, and Picturesque, why not more picturesque? Some authorities refuse to believe that such extensive construction had no utilitarian basis, perhaps for industry, or defence, or religious ritual. Was it built from scratch, or adapted from some other use? Could it really be late Tudor/early Stuart – from the time of Bishop Anthony Rudd or his 'ingenious' son Sir Rice? At the eleventh hour, after much confusion, this seemed increasingly likely.

We must explore the possibilities by meeting some of the characters of the past. Our 'history lesson' today looks at the era when the Rudds occupied the stage at Aberglasney. As we meet the four (or five?) successive generations of this family, we speculate (as the experts have done) what contribution each was capable of making to the property. Did any of them have the means and the vision and the motive to create the strange Cloister Garden, and for what purpose was it intended? And not just the garden. By the reign of Charles II Aberglasney mansion ranked among the greatest houses in the county, as we shall see. Vaulting ambition was at work; it is one of Aberglasney's ironies that by the time that assessment was made, the Rudds were already in steep decline.

With Bishop Rudd we are in the age of Shakespeare. Although the Bishop himself remains a rather shadowy figure, there is a sense of humanity about him. It feels easy to identify with him over one point: it seems that he, like so many others, fell completely under the spell of this lovely spot. For someone who had lived all over England and moved in the highest circles in the land to elect to be buried beside his wife in the parish church at Llangathen, hard by Aberglasney, must be significant (it is as unusual as his declining to be buried with his predecessors-in-office in his great cathedral of St David's in Pembrokeshire). It suggests that Llangathen was the place that Bishop Rudd and his lady in their mature years had eventually come to consider as home.

Both in person and in legend, Bishop Rudd has become completely enmeshed in the history of Aberglasney. His story shows him to have been an extraordinary man – in one instance, at least, a 'turbulent priest'.

Anthony, the eldest son in the lively family of one Leonard Rudd, was born in Easby, Yorkshire in about 1548.[2] He was sent to Cambridge, where he took his BA in 1566, his MA in 1570 and the degree of Bachelor of Divinity in 1577. He briefly held a living at Shudy Camps in Cambridgeshire, but rose to be made Dean of Gloucester in 1584. Moving ever westwards he was consecrated Bishop of St David's in June 1594. He evidently accumulated wealth as he gained status. By general consensus he was a bright man – a most admirable preacher – and was earmarked to succeed John Whitgift as the next Archbishop of Canterbury until 1596, when he put his foot right in it with a Lenten sermon he preached to Elizabeth I at Richmond. This brought a speedy end to his hopes of the desired archbishopric and his enjoyment of the Queen's favour – but it brings him a key role in our Aberglasney story. A marginal note puts it in a nutshell: 'The Bishop, by plain preaching, gains the Queen's favour. And by too personal preaching, loseth it again.'[3]

Little is known of the character of the Bishop, or of the details of his personal life, and so it is somewhat paradoxical that the one scene in which we find Anthony Rudd appearing in close-up takes place on the most celebrated stage in Christendom, the Court of Queen Elizabeth I. Sharing the spotlight with the Queen herself, but starring as villain of the piece, is our good Bishop Rudd.

Rudd had been assured that plain sermons were most pleasing to the Queen, and on 28 March Rudd duly took as his text Psalms 90:12 ('So teach us to number our days, that we may apply our hearts unto wisdom'). But you didn't mention time to the ageing queen. 'To remark to her the progress of time was to wound her in the tenderest part, and not even from her ghostly counsellors would she endure a topic so offensive as the mention of her age.'[4] Rudd's remarks upon 'the most reverend age of my most deare and dread Soveraigne', allusions to how age had 'furrowed her face and bespeckled her hair with its meal' and other observations of a temporal character were far too near the bone.

Worse, if anything: in the manner of the time Bishop Rudd made great play with the significance of some sacred and auspicious numbers. He spoke of three for the Trinity, seven for the Sabbath, seven-times-seven for a Jubilee – and was approaching seven-times-nine for the climacteric year, when something in the Queen's look pulled him up short. Her age was precisely sixty-three. Rudd rapidly changed tack and tried to make amends, bringing in a handful of other less personally relevant numbers (citing 666, with which he could prove the pope an Antichrist, and the ill-omened eighty-eight, the year in which 'all things fell out prosperously for her Highness' and when the Armada had been vanquished), but the damage had been done. The Queen muttered that he should have kept his arithmetic to himself and went off in a huff.

Bishop Rudd remained rusticated at home for a few days on the advice of the Lord

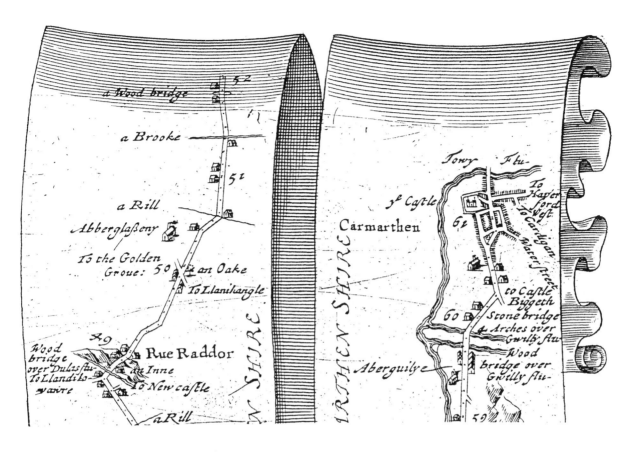

Keeper, appealing to Sir Robert Cecil and to the Council to mediate on his behalf with
Her Majesty. He claimed he had merely hoped to 'encourage her in well doing, even by
those speeches which proved so offensive'. But it was to no avail: he had burned his
boats. The Queen in fact was soon back in conspicuously good spirits, demonstrating
to those around her how keen her sight and other faculties were – 'Only to show how
the good Bishop was deceived in supposing she was so decayed in her limbs and senses
as himself perhaps and others of that age were wont to be', as Sir John Harington put
it. She even rebuked someone who spoke slightingly of Rudd and his sermon.

Bishop Rudd kept a low profile in public for the remaining seven years of Elizabeth's
reign, and the offending sermon was published only after her death. (Three later
sermons that Bishop Rudd preached before James I apparently passed without incident,
and his son became one of the King's favourites.) Given the capricious nature of the
Queen's temper the Bishop probably got off lightly. He still considered himself in
disgrace in 1597. But in the same year, we find him achieving a more worldly kind of
honour, obtaining a new grant of arms and relinquishing the ancient arms of the
Rudds.[5] It is intriguing to find the Bishop seeking this kind of status symbol for himself:
it has been suggested that he wanted to found a new branch of the family that would
eclipse the old, humbler order. He evidently had a sense of self-importance, and wanted
it publically recognized. His arms can be seen decorating the splendid tomb erected to
his memory in Llangathen parish church – itself a monumental advertisement for
Bishop Rudd's eminence, and an indication that the place eventually became important
to him. However, in 1597 he was by no means committed to a new life in Wales. Not

yet. In 1601–2 we find him petitioning Sir Robert Cecil to be a means for his translation to the See of Hereford. Less than a year later he writes again from his palace at Abergwili in an attempt to secure a move:

> Having been heretofore suitor to you for my translation hence to Hereford, I do now renew the same petition, with the addition that if I cannot obtain Hereford, yet I may be removed to Norwich, upon my faithful promise that I will be dutifull to you during life.[6]

To no avail. In the eyes of the world the change in Bishop Rudd's fortune might seem for the worse: Carmarthen looks like a poor substitute for Canterbury. But to find himself in Wales for the remaining years of his life was not, perhaps, such a hardship. The see of St David's was among the richest. It had several fine palaces, including one at St David's in Pembrokeshire and the one at Abergwili on the northern fringes of Carmarthen, ten miles downriver from Llangathen. In a mutually beneficial relationship he is reported to have 'wrought much on the Welsh by his wisdom and won their affection' as well as to have built up an estate for his children 'by moderate thrift' and by leases of ecclesiastical property. Like many career churchmen in the generations following the Reformation, Bishop Rudd succeeded in establishing his household as a new gentry family in the county. It seems that he purchased Aberglasney as a home of his own. The long-accepted version of the story goes something like this:

> The Bishop purchased an estate in the Parish of Llangathen, about twelve miles from Carmarthen, called Aberglasney, and there he erected a handsome seat in the Elizabethan style. He probably pulled down an earlier mansion or castle to carry out his plans, for on the lawn to this day is to be seen an ancient entrance gateway of some three hundred years earlier, and the lines of the present raised terrace walk certainly appear to be those of an ancient fortress wall.[7]

This view from 1920 goes on to note that great changes had been made in the structure of the house over the years. It has to be said that sceptics remain doubtful that Rudd's house was actually Aberglasney, and it is a fact that no conclusive evidence has yet surfaced: what we need is miraculously to discover something like an authentic signed letter from the bishop headed 'Aberglasney, Tuesday. . .' and ideally expressing his satisfaction at the effect of 'ye cloister walls'.

The mystery is compounded by the fact that documents known to have existed comparatively recently have disappeared. Rudd family papers dating back to the late sixteenth century contained accounts relating to building work undertaken by the bishop, apparently at Aberglasney. In the 1950s these papers were removed from Aberglasney when the Evans family sold the property; they were subsequently stolen

RIGHT *Bishop Rudd and his lady lie in the parish church of Llangathen in a 'bedstead' tomb of unparalleled splendour hereabouts. The heavy draperies are beautifully carved and the classical canopy is impressive though dilapidated. This surveyor's record of the figures in plan gives only the faintest hint of the majesty of the monument – like the stave of notes representing the basic theme of a brilliant concerto.*

in peculiar circumstances. In the 1960s Mrs Eric Evans, who had remarried and was now Mrs Lyndon Skeggs, was approached by a man who claimed to be the Royal Calligrapher and who asked to borrow the Rudd papers. Convinced of his *bona fides*, she let him take them away. Neither he nor the papers have ever been seen again.

The circumstantial evidence for assuming that the Bishop lived at Aberglasney is, however, strong. We do know that he owned various pieces of land in Llangathen including Lanlash, the property due west of Aberglasney in the valley bottom of the River Lash, just off the main A40 trunk road. Neither this nor any other Llangathen house of the time would seem to rival a place like Aberglasney as a suitable seat for someone of his standing. Lanlash is mentioned specifically and separately in his will (where he bequeathed 'his implements of husbandry at his house at Llangathen and Llanlash Loyds at his death. . .'). His will ordered that many of his personal effects be carried 'to his house in Llangathen' for the benefit of his widow during her lifetime. And his successors were quite simply 'of Aberglasney'. An early account states that Bishop Rudd 'built a hansome seat (with a very decent chapel with a curious pulpit,

ornamented with painted glass) called Aberglasney.'[8] The conclusion is that he bought or acquired the estate from a member of the Thomas family around 1600 and greatly altered and extended the house that they had occupied. The precise extent of his lands in Llangathen is not known, but he acquired further properties in Carmarthenshire in the early 1600s, adding up to a considerable amount in total. He provided for his family and extended his charity to the poorer members of his flock, in his will founding an almshouse in Carmarthen. He was buried in Llangathen parish church and the splendid 'bedstead' monument erected in 1616 to the memory of him and his wife is there still.

If Bishop Rudd rebuilt and extended a house at Llangathen it must have been to accommodate his retinue, to entertain visitors and as a public demonstration of his status – conspicuous construction rather than consumption – rather than to house a growing number of children and grandchildren, for his immediate family was rather small. The Bishop would have been approaching fifty when he came to Wales, and the handful of offspring of whom we are aware seems to have been born when he was well into his forties. What members of the Rudd family might we picture in residence at Aberglasney?

Bishop Rudd's wife was born Anne Dalton and came from Thurnham in Lancashire. The tomb in Llangathen Church is attended by four weepers, two boys and two girls. (If the figures attending the tomb are intended to represent the incumbents' offspring, as is often the case, the girls presumably died in infancy.) Two sons concern us. The eldest, Anthony, was born in 1590 during the time when the Reverend Anthony Rudd was Dean of Gloucester, and matriculated at Magdalen College, Oxford, in 1603. In due course he married Margaret Symms, said to be 'a lady of considerable fortune in the county of Gloucester'. They had no children, and although he inherited his father's estate, he was dead by 1620. A second son, Rice (sometimes named in documents as Richard: perhaps the child was christened Richard but became familiarly known as Rice), was designated executor of his father's will but became sole heir and brought to the estate a baronetcy. He is a key figure in the story of Aberglasney.

We don't seem to have a date of birth for the future Sir Rice. He was under age when his father made his will in January 1614, which puts his date of birth no earlier than 1594 – the year Anthony Rudd became Bishop of St David's. It is tempting to speculate that perhaps he was born after Anthony Rudd acceded to the bishopric and came to Wales. If so he might have spent large parts of his formative years at Llangathen. One factor in favour of this theory is his Welsh Christian name. Rice is an Anglicization of the Welsh Rhys, and, incidentally, a name closely connected both with Aberglasney and with Dynevor.[9] The Rudd household would certainly have socialized with the well-born neighbour, Walter Rice, who was knighted by James I in 1603 and was the local MP. There was possibly a common interest in building: Sir Walter was at the time actively improving Newton House on the Dynevor estate.

We must keep a weather eye on the question of building, because it is crucial to deciphering the mystery of Aberglasney's cloisters. Archaeologists' finds date different phases of construction to the first half of the seventeenth century – spot on for the period when the first two Rudd incumbents were most upwardly mobile, and also a time when wealthy householders all over Britain were building themselves fine residences laced about with terrace walks, arcades and other garden structures. The Earl of Exeter's great Elizabethan house at Wimbledon in Surrey had spectacular arcaded terraces adding to the drama of its entrance. And some of the most sophisticated English gardens of the early seventeenth century like Wilton, Moor Park and Hadham Hall (Hertfordshire) had terraces built upon arcades and colonnades. Houses in Wales with similarly Italianate features include St Donat's (South Glamorgan) and Raglan (Gwent). Aberglasney is only exceptional in that its cloisters and archways survive.

Their stylistic confusion is another matter, and we will hear what the experts have to say about this in more detail later. The brutish functionality of the side ranges puts the visitor in mind of fortifications. Or maybe in the garden's prime this grimmer aspect was eclipsed by other, more ostentatious features since disappeared, like summer-houses or banqueting houses crowning the more elegant western arcade, and who knows what other structures. Perhaps the inspiration was sheer theatre. The reign of James I was, after all, the era of masques by Inigo Jones *et al*. Aberglasney's Jacobean residents frequented that James's court. We know James was keen on gardens. We know the Bishop had a foothold; we know his son was one of the King's numberless 'favourites'. Enter Rice Rudd the first.

If Bishop Rudd first made Wales his home, his heir seems to have become more deeply involved in the principality, particularly in their adoptive Carmarthenshire – a comparatively rich and productive county commended in 1610 by John Speed for being 'not altogether so pestered by hills as her bordering neighbours are'. It sounds as if Rice Rudd in the succeeding generation considered himself a Welshman. He alone amongst the Bishop's branch of the family managed by siring five or six offspring to found anything like a dynasty, although he too lost his eldest son. His two wives belonged to eminent Welsh families, and his children married into the local gentry. He gave one of his sons the stirring Welsh name of Urien, after the king whose fame is the main theme of the poems of Taliesin.[10] His first wife, Jane Rhys, died in 1626. His second marriage, to Elizabeth, daughter of Sir Thomas Aubrey of Llantrithyd in Glamorgan, was childless. However, it brought Sir Rice into contact with the Aubreys (relatives of the antiquarian John Aubrey), whose new house and gardens at Llantrithyd, as we shall see, bear interesting echoes of Aberglasney's.

Rice Rudd was active in public life, serving as High Sheriff of Carmarthenshire in 1619 and again in 1636. But he also moved freely in Court circles. He is described as a close friend of James I. His estate was enhanced in 1616–17 by a patent from King James granting him valuable favours.[11] His status was further enhanced when Charles I honoured him with a baronetcy in 1628. In the same year Sir Rice's near neighbour at Golden Grove, Sir John Vaughan (who had served as Comptroller of the Household of Charles when Prince of Wales), was made Earl of Carbery. Being based in rural Wales did not mean being a nonentity. The county town of Carmarthen was a thriving, bustling economic centre in Sir Rice's day: even after the Civil War, Jeremy Taylor, a visitor at Golden Grove, could describe it as 'one of the plentifulest towns that I ever set foot in. . .there is nothing scare, dear or hard to come by but tobacco pipes'. We find Sir Rice active there in 1640 furthering the charitable bequest initiated by his parents in endowing 'Bishop Rudd's Hospitalle and Almeshouse'.

Up to this point we can picture Aberglasney as a flourishing, growing, fashionable place. However, the family fortunes were not secure. The Civil War brought desecration to the Bishop's tomb (in an incident that gave rise to another Llangathen ghost story) and damage to the Baronet's pocket. Like most of the Welsh gentry, Sir Rice supported the Royalists and, like them, afterwards was subjected to heavy parliamentary fines. He had to pay the considerable sum of £581 12s. 7d. Such penalties hastened the decline of many members of the lesser gentry, without capital to invest and so dependent for their income upon rents and sales of the produce from their lands, and many now mortgaged their estates up to the hilt. It may be from this period that the deep financial problems of the Rudds of Aberglasney stemmed. Had they fatally overstretched themselves in building their splendid new house? It was evidently quite exceptional, as we shall hear.

Some notion of the relative importance of places like Aberglasney after the Restoration comes from the assessment for hearth tax or 'chimney money' imposed by Charles II. Householders in England and Wales were required to pay two shillings per annum for every fireplace in their possession. Suddenly we have a useful league table of dwellings for the year 1670, and what it reveals about Aberglasney's status is remarkable. A decent farmstead like Aberglasney's next-door neighbour Berllandywyll might have four hearths; Brynhafod, also in Llangathen parish, had five. The bishop's palace at Abergwili was a more imposing residence, rated at eleven hearths. Once fireplaces could be counted in double figures you were in a new league. Relatively few Carmarthenshire houses were this important but Aberglasney ranked with Golden Grove in the very top echelon: each was rated as having no fewer than thirty hearths.[12] In building their stately pile the Rudds had put themselves at the top of the pile. They also had to fork out £3 a year in hearth money for their grand house.

But thereby – to one of those hearths at Aberglasney – hangs a terrible tale.

In Sir Rice Rudd's household originated the haunting story of the ill-fated maids who all died in their beds one night. It is tied up with the superstition that the appearance of a ghostly candle presages someone's imminent death. In Aberglasney's case the number of candles and deaths is variously given as three, five, six, seven or even nine but the specific details in the earliest printed account, 'confirmed by divers Persons of good Quality and Reputation', have a ring of accuracy. The report came from a vicar, the Reverend John Davis, who attributed the story to his wife's sister, one 'Jane Wyat', nurse to Baronet Rudd's 'three eldest children' after their mother's death:

> . . .his House-keeper going late into a Chamber where the Maid Servants lay, saw five of these Lights together; a while after that Chamber being newly plaistred, a great Grate of Coal Fire was kindled therein to hasten the drying of it. At Night five of the Maid Servants went there to Bed as they were wont, and in the Morning were all found dead and suffocated with the Steam of the new tempered Lime and Coal.[13]

One can imagine the scene as the following morning dawns in the newly refurbished house at Aberglasney. The Baronet is perhaps away, at Carmarthen or at Court (or even courting a new wife?), but the household wakes to find the hearths dirty and the fires unlit. There is no water heating in the kitchen. Irritated, even angry, the housekeeper or the nurse storms upstairs to the attic room which we assume these lowly persons were assigned: maidservants were usually kept well out of possible contact with ostlers, garden boys and other male hands. And then the realization – perhaps first some sickly smell lingering in the chamber before the discovery of one, two, three, all of the wretched little bodies stark and still. Who wouldn't shiver at the thought, let alone the sight? Who wouldn't wonder for a moment if Aberglasney and its ambitious owners were not starred by ill-luck?

The 'corpse candles' phenomenon has fired the popular imagination hereabouts. It has local origins, being closely associated with south-west Wales and with Bishop Rudd's own diocese – the See of St David's – in particular: it was supposed to derive from the patron saint David himself, who prayed for such intimations of mortality to instil some fear of the life to come into his wandering flock. Mr Davis, who seems to be the source of the tradition at Aberglasney, added in a cheerfully matter-of-fact tone, 'not that we see anything besides the Light, but yet it resembles a material Candle-light as much as Eggs do Eggs, only they sometimes appear and instantly disappear'. Just recently one of the last owners of the house offered a perfectly prosaic explanation of her sighting of flickering lights – as we shall hear when we meet her in our last chapter.

The only Baronet Rudd to live at Aberglasney with a number of small children was Sir Rice, and the statement that this took place after the death of their mother – which we know to have been in 1626   pinpoints the tragic event to perhaps sometime around 1630. But things are never that simple.

We now set out on a detour which takes us far in time from the Rudds and for a moment away from the cloisters – in fact, we move indoors, back into the mansion, which we usually treat simply as the backdrop to our garden explorations. But the saga of the maids has had a sort of butterfly effect on fantasy and fact at Aberglasney, and it is part of our story to trace some of those fluctuations.

Another version of the tale has the ghosts of six young girls walking the grounds of Aberglasney, and the deaths rather more recent. 'The girls were maids at the big house who had decorated their bedroom as a surprise for their master and mistress and, sleeping with the doors and windows shut tight, they suffocated from the fumes of lead paint in the Blue Room. . .'.[14] It seems unlikely that maids would take it upon themselves to paint a room 'as a surprise' and then sleep in it themselves. Somewhere along the line the specific detail of the blue paint and of the lead poisoning has crept in, which smacks of an embellishment from the nineteenth century. Was there perhaps an actual reprise of the tragedy in some form, or are we looking at another case of Aberglasney's Chinese whispers? The tale takes on new slants in the era of the Gothick novel. A

Victorian descendant of the Dyers gave a concise version, with three ghosts, but back in the Bishop's era: 'Bishop Rudd from his study observed three lights moving out of the Hall entrance door, a short time before three servant girls were killed by a charcoal fire.'[15] A modern-day account, placing the event in the Philipps era of the early nineteenth century, when the house was undoubtedly being spruced up, relates that 'seven maid servants were found dead in their beds inside the Blue Room'. The Blue Room again. People around today who visited or worked in the house can tell you precisely where the Blue Room was. 'It was claimed toxic fumes from the lime mortar plaster had percolated from the walls and asphyxiated them in their sleep.'[16]

The incident has entered legend but still has very real repercussions. The artist Nigel Hughes, commissioned to design sculptures for the restored garden, heard the story in the summer of 1998 on a research trip to Aberglasney and casually speculated that the paint might have been Paris Green, also known as Emerald Green. This brilliant pigment is copper aceto-arsenite, which could make arsenic poisoning the cause of death (it was also used in the perilous past as an insecticide). His innocent suggestion gave the story a new sci-fi twist by setting up potential alarm bells among the team involved in restoring the house: Health and Safety measures were rapidly put into effect to analyse samples of any greenish wall coatings found indoors. Even if it had been repeatedly painted over, a material so toxic might be dangerous to contractors who unknowingly handled it. Paris Green seemed a red herring when research showed that the pigment dated only from the 1780s[17] – too late to have been the fatal substance that killed Baronet Rudd's maids at Aberglasney in the early 1630s. The cautionary mood nevertheless prevailed in the house; might some zealous decorator preparing rooms at Aberglasney in around 1805 for the arrival of Thomas Phillips from India not have taken a fancy to an arrestingly lurid shade of green, and introduced a fine layer of this fatal cocktail to some room somewhere in the house?

With the sort of crazy logic you get at Aberglasney, none of the chronology works; the detail is dodgy (blue, green? isn't colour in the eye of the beholder?) – but the drama remains. Sure enough, contractors found dull green paint containing arsenic in two different rooms and a passageway. Some of it was in such dangerously high concentration that special procedures for its controlled removal had to be instigated – the stuff had to be treated as if was asbestos. Via specially drawn up Risk Assessments and Method Statements, workmen wearing what looked like space-suits in a sealed-off area bagged up the contaminated render and paint, and it was disposed of as toxic waste. Here was ancient Aberglasney making groundbreaking modern history for the building industry.

Back to the 1600s. This storyteller is sticking to that early version as the gospel from which later apocrypha sprang. (Unless there was *another* set of Blue-Room deaths in the nineteenth century?) The constant element in the various versions of the tale of the maids is the fact that rebuilding and/or decorating was involved. This is of interest to us, because it confirms our suspicion that Sir Rice Rudd in about the third decade of the seventeenth century was actively engaged in improving and maybe expanding his residence. There is even a hint in some versions that the work was being done with almost undue haste: why the urgency for the maids to use the room before it was ready? And was that a new mistress – a new Lady Rudd – that he was bringing home for the first time?

We are, of course, at the same time concerned and curious about those poor maids, sleeping in a room where the plaster was still damp – and then paying for this with their lives. The direct cause of their death is attributable not to the lime plaster, however, but to the presence of that 'great Grate of Coal Fire' and carbon monoxide poisoning. 'If the flue was small, or short, it would not be able to cope with an unusually large, banked up fire,' says expert Rory Young, consultant conservator of historic buildings.[18] 'Downdrafts could push gases down into the room, or maybe there were gaps round doors into attics that were full of fumes from leaking stacks running up through them.' If extensive building work was in progress it could be that not only were various rooms being plastered, but chimneys and fireplaces were undergoing alteration or being newly created. In the haste to have the house made ready, there was no time to check that all was in order and that the flues were drawing efficiently before the fatal fire was lit.

If Sir Rice was busy refurbishing his mansion in order to impress Elizabeth Aubrey, was he also, perhaps, making elaborate improvements to his grounds? If he had visited the Aubreys' seat at Llantrithyd Place in Glamorgan – one of the finest houses in the county – he would surely have been impressed by the complex gardens laid out in the late sixteenth century to complement a slightly earlier house.[19] Today that garden is in decay, but its description rings faint bells at Aberglasney: 'Two walled terraces descend from the churchyard to rectilinear fishponds linked by a canalized, stone-lined stream, in the valley bottom. From the north-east corner of the house a raised walk leads down into the gardens, over a bridge (now collapsed, but formerly over a walk leading to the terraces), past the fishponds, and up ruined steps to a raised look-out platform or gazebo.'[20] The extensive earthworks and stone walkway 'testify to the modish taste' of Llantrithyd's owners.[21] 'There is little to compare the quality of cultural milieux, scale or functions between Llantrithyd and the walkway at Aberglasney,' wrote one sceptic.[22] But it seems that Aberglasney's owners, albeit perhaps on a more modest scale, had similarly modish tastes.

Thomas Wotton in *English Baronets* described Sir Rice as 'an ingenious and learned man'. Ingenious is one of those words that has become debased: in the seventeenth century it had a specific and stronger resonance, not merely clever, but 'having an aptitude for invention or construction'. Sir Rice had something in common with his distinguished kinsman Thomas Rudd of Higham Ferrers (1583–1656), an expert in engineering coastal defences and military fortifications for his king in the very years

RIGHT *By the time the Aberglasney Restoration Trust came on the scene the parapet structures to the west of the house were engulfed in vegetation. They formed the three sides of a square closed on the fourth by the mansion's west façade, but they looked more like fragments of disused railway embankment than anything else.*

LEFT *The greatest bane was the head-high tangle of brambles and Japanese knotweed, which prevented anyone from walking across the garden at ground level.*

The arches: before clearing and restoration

RIGHT *Speculation abounded about the possible utility of the arches: few believed that they could have been part of an ornamental garden layout. Although they were right beside a once-fashionable house, they prompted people to think of lime kilns, a tanner's yard or store rooms for wool and fleeces. Others suggested a monastery or a fort.*

LEFT *Some variation could be detected in the shapes of the arches, and a couple of them provided passageways into adjacent garden areas, which could be closed off by rusting iron gates.*

RIGHT *The yews flanking the way to the Pool Garden were an apple of discord between clashing restorationists: to preserve or to remove? Irish yews date only from 1760, and these were growing well above the level of the excavated Stuart garden, so they were given the chop.*

The arches: support for the western range

RIGHT *The roots of seedling yews – as well as ivies and other invaders – are partly responsible for undermining the fabric of the walls. Hardly visible at the end of the parapet is a mature yew whose confusion of branches suggest it was once shaped or topiarized in some way.*

LEFT *By the 1990s parts of the western range were precarious. The external stone cladding was bulging away from the rubble core (to which it had been poorly tied in), and was even falling away in places. Emergency measures included erecting shoring timber to hold things in place until rebuilding work could begin.*

The arches: progress on the parapet walls

LEFT *As repair work made systematic progress along the western range, the raking shores of timber that prevented serious collapse could be removed section by section. The parapet walls were dismantled stone by stone ready to be rebuilt to the original height. Although the builders reused existing stone, some additional material had to be brought in.*

BELOW *It took a great deal of care to make sure that rebuilt sections of wall matched in perfectly with parts that were sound enough to need only repointing. Beforehand the contractors tried out a number of lime mortar mixes, varying ingredients and proportions until the resulting tone and texture achieved the effect the architect intended.*

LEFT *The arcaded walk between the Cloister Garden and the Pool sinks into a morass of vegetation. The seedlings on the top of this western range are a particular problem as their deep roots penetrate the layer of puddled clay that acts as a seal over the walkway below. Yet it is possible that plants (and even shrubs) were once grown bordering the pathway. A Gardeners Chronicle account of Aberglasney in 1892 describes how 'a second broad walk with garden beds as borders, is carried over the walk below'.*

The arches: progress

RIGHT *In 1992 archaeologist Lesley Howes was commissioned to do a structural survey of the 'parapet structures'. Here Leslie Capon, a member of her team, makes a stone-by-stone scale drawing of one of the arches in the west range. Comparison of such records might reveal different styles or phases of building.*

RIGHT *The northern parapet walk in its sorriest state. It was smothered with weeds whose roots allowed water into the rubble core. Many of the capping stones had been stolen. It took detective work to establish what to aim for in rebuilding. Just enough of the original remained to establish levels, and to locate the slightly bizarre distribution of the unusual ornate crenellations.*

LEFT *If Aberglasney's walls once hosted an excess of vegetation, the rebuilt structures can seem almost too squeaky clean. A seed-bank of colonizers stands ready to rectify the balance. Along with lichens, dainty wall ferns and trails of ivy-leaved toadflax may be welcomed, but ivy itself will be treated with caution, and maybe with glyphosate.*

LEFT AND RIGHT *The view from the south Cloister Walk shows how the inner parapet is lower than the outer one (left): it just reaches the scoop of the half-moon crenellations. These were shaped from the sort of timber 'centre' that is used to build arches, in this case inverted. The repaired parapets (right) were handsomely capped with riven slabs of greenish sandstone with fettled edges.*

The arches: the cryptoporticus

ABOVE *The climax of the Cloister Garden is the long arcaded walkway in the western range, opposite the mansion, which rejoices in the name of cryptoporticus. Like the long gallery of an Elizabethan house, it offers an invitation to stroll up and down taking exercise.*

when a great deal of building must have taken place at Aberglasney. This Thomas Rudd is primarily of interest to Aberglasney because his only child Judith married the bishop's grandson and namesake. He was singled out in 1627 by Charles I as 'chief engineer of all castles, forts and fortifications within Wales'. 1628 was the year in which Charles I knighted Rice Rudd, and it is hard to believe the kinsmen were not in contact around this time if not before, both at Court and in Wales. Speculation conjures visions of Thomas lending a hand in building at Aberglasney, but the structures do not look like the work of the highly professional surveyor who wrote books on practical geometry and military matters. They have the roughness of a design drawn on the back of an envelope or imperfectly remembered by one who was no draughtsman.

Before we return to our family history we should perhaps lay those poor maidservants to rest. They remain as anonymous today as they were over three centuries ago. Llangathen parish church and its churchyard are studded with the stacked-up names of Aberglasney's illustrious owners and their families – carved into plaques, memorials, headstones and monuments of every style. We have no names for the maids. We are not even sure where they lie. Some parishioners will point to a row of plain slate-slabbed graves near the church, but the vicar, the Reverend Roger Hughes, says these are nineteenth-century burials. He leads you to a spot shaded by immense old yews and a newer cherry laurel near the northernmost gate to the churchyard where an old parishioner once assured him the five maids are buried, as her predecessors had assured her. Here alongside the path we find a series of coffin-shapes outlined in a crude mixture of pieces of sawn slate and of everyday split roofing slates. Count them: three nearest the church are clearly visible, but then there is a gap, and another, incomplete set of slate outlining that is less distinctly a grave. Even here the numbers defy our attempts to count them.

History does not reveal to us the reaction of Sir Rice and his household to the tragedy of the maids any more than to the death of his first wife, or later to that of his eldest son. To lose a relatively young wife was not uncommon in those days, and maids were even easier to replace. With his five, or six, children, a new well-connected wife and his career in public office, Sir Rice looked all set to establish a Rudd dynasty at Llangathen. Four of his children made good marriages, two of his daughters tightening the bonds

The term 'cloister' need not imply a monastery or church, experts say, but these cloisters may have been planned by a bishop. This range dates from around 1600, when Bishop Rudd is supposed to have acquired Aberglasney. Rather than ecclesiastical, his model is likely to have been the

of kinship by marrying into the families of his wives.[23] But it is the boys who are relevant, because they carry the succession. A younger son, Thomas (whose son Anthony eventually became the third baronet) married an Aberglasney neighbour[24] but eventually settled at Capel Evan.

Sir Rice Rudd's eldest son, born in 1619 – so presumably one of those 'three eldest children' cared for by nurse Jane Wyat – was another Anthony. Apart from that brief early appearance at Aberglasney, the action of his short life takes place off-stage for us. We find him matriculating at Oxford in 1635 and marrying in 1640 – marrying, as we said, Judith Rudd, the only child and heiress of his father's friend and kinsman Thomas. Alas! the heir

Renaissance-inspired secular buildings that his contemporaries were erecting in great numbers. Many of them had raised and arcaded walkways like these.

to Aberglasney died before he was thirty as the country lapsed into the second phase of the Civil War. His will of 1648 prayed for peace 'for this distracted kingdome and Churche' as well as begging for God's blessing on his two 'tender children', a daughter named Mary and a son named Rice (born around 1643), who would succeed his grandfather as second baronet in 1664. Young Anthony Rudd should have prayed for peace in his own immediate family, for eventually this too was 'distracted' – torn apart – by the acrimonious lawsuits that followed his widow's remarriage and must be partly to blame for the family's eventual loss of Aberglasney.

His son, the second Rice Rudd, is a paradox, and an elusive figure. We find him active here in Carmarthenshire, we find him busy there in Northamptonshire, holding public office for each in turn. During his ownership Aberglasney's fame reached its apogée (perhaps because he was the assessor who counted its thirty hearths in 1670?) and yet in his hands it was soon mortgaged away. Was he in some way to blame for this loss, allowing his fortune to trickle away in electioneering expenses? Were family squabbles about land to blame? Or had the fines of the Civil War irrevocably punctured the Aberglasney bubble?

He starts out as a Londoner during his minority, the ward of Charles Cornwallis of High Holborn. Around 1661 he marries Cornwallis's daughter Dorothy, who brought with her a portion of £1000.[25] Despite his metropolitan connections, he takes an active part in public life in Wales. But through his mother's and his sister's marriages to Pembertons he becomes embroiled in the affairs of Higham Ferrers.[26] Somehow Sir Rice loses what fortune the family still possesses. Received wisdom is that he expended huge sums on unsuccessful electioneering, although whether in Wales or in Northamptonshire is not specified: the latter, perhaps, since it is in 1682 that he began to lose his grip on his properties. In due course he mortgaged Aberglasney. Just before his death he directed that his estate in Higham Ferrers was to be sold to pay debts, and should the money thus realized prove insufficient, then the Aberglasney estate was to be sold as well. He died in 1701 in London – 'festooned in debt', intestate, childless. He was brought back to Llangathen for burial.[27]

A few sentences will sweep the remaining Rudds out of the picture. With the death of the second Sir Rice the title passed to a cousin, another Anthony, whose father Thomas Rudd of Capel Evan was the youngest son of the first baronet. Finding it immensely difficult to get hold of his debt-ridden inheritance, he instituted an action early in 1705 in the High Court of Chancery to try to recover possession, apparently without success; he died in 1706. Sir Anthony was succeeded by his infant son Sir John, born in about 1704, who became the fourth baronet. Sir John died without issue in 1739, bringing to an end the male line of the Rudds of Aberglasney. But their connection with the place was already long over.[28] In the meantime, in June 1710 Aberglasney and other parts of the Carmarthenshire estate had been sold by the Hon. Thomas Watson Wentworth, a mortgagee, to Robert Dyer. We look forward to being formally introduced to Robert Dyer in the next chapter. Before we move on, let's quickly take a closer look at those famed 'enigmatic structures' that surround us in the Cloister Garden, and hear some of the speculations that they have engendered.

The enclosure lies to the side of the house, to the south-west. The land slopes gently away in this direction before sweeping up again into the dramatic profile of Grongar Hill some half a mile away: this is Aberglasney's most prized vista. It was what you saw from the windows of the best rooms, and what draws the eye from the parapet walk. For convenience in describing what is there, the pundits and puzzlers assume that the house is square-on to the compass and facing north, and that the courtyard lies to the west of the house. On three sides it is surrounded by the elevated walk built up on irregular stone arches of loosely jointed masonry: the house itself forms the fourth side, but is detached – it does not physically quite close the square. The west range of the walk is parallel to the house and the south range is aligned with the south façade of the house. The north range, however, is slightly further north than the front of the house (an instance of asymmetry that perplexes those who would like the whole to have been conceived and built as a geometric entity). The west range is tunnel-vaulted with nine visible arched openings facing eastwards, into the garden. One of these arches – the largest, central one – leads through the terrace to the Pond Garden below and provides a welcome glimpse of the outside world beyond. Another, smaller one is aligned along the north range.

Enclosed chambers occupy the north and south corners, where the west range abuts the two side ranges. The chamber in the south-west corner retains some rendering internally and has crude openings or windows. The north-west chamber has a doorway with a pointed arch, built into the north range. The south range consists of a solid external wall against the Upper Walled Garden (where the ground level is higher than that within the courtyard garden) with five chambers, and one additional arched opening to the west, facing into the garden. Three of these arches were partially or completely blocked at some stage. The north range also has five arches into the garden. Here the profiles are more regular and have outward openings at each end towards the north. The profiles and construction of the archways vary greatly: this is simply not very precise architecture, more back-of-an-envelope, amateurish stuff. To give an idea of size: the sunken garden within the enclosure makes a broad oblong that you could just about squeeze three tennis courts cheek-by-jowl into, provided you skimped a little on the back-court area. It all slopes gently downwards from the house.

The terrace walk or parapet walk around the three sides is quite wide enough to accommodate the flowing skirts of farthingales and crinolines. The broad parapet edging makes it a comfortable height for sitting. The outer parapet walls of the north and west sides of the ranges are ornamented with unusual semicircular indentations or crenellations at regular intervals. Access to the raised walk appeared to be via ramps near the house but, as archaeology has revealed, was once by means of steps. Here is one key to the enigma. Beneath its obscuring layers of decay and neglect, the garden inherited by the Restoration Trust was essentially a Victorian one (incidentally, in highly fashionable Jacobean style), overlying and masking the original. As restoration began in earnest, first the Victorian garden was denuded of its mantle of vegetation, and was recognized as a period cover-up: then the serious digging could begin. Meantime garden historians delved in the archives and sifted the evidence on site.

A handful of recent commentators suggested these Cloister Garden structures must have had some utilitarian origin, since they look so very unprepossessing. A store for fleeces, said one. A tannery, someone proposed – not without a shred of reason, since (as well as Dyers) members of Aberglasney's families have been tanners. (A reminder that the smell of the urine used in the process would not be tolerated so close to a gentleman's seat quashed this theory.) Someone likened the arches to a row of lime kilns. Another suggestion was that the structure had been modified from an earlier defensive building. An advertisement when the house was put up to let in 1872 briskly describes 'a three-sided Terrace Walk, constructed on the walls of an ancient fortress'.

Another fallacy held sway for most of the twentieth century: that Aberglasney was once the site of an abbey or priory of some kind. The round-headed arches put people in mind of cloisters, or monks' cells, and they assumed that Aberglasney had monastic origins. This was the view of Colonel Mayhew, Aberglasney's owner at the turn of the century, who had been convinced by an expert on church architecture that the entrance gateway was Romanesque and dated from the early Norman period; he reported in 1905 that he was doubtful about the location of the main building, but speculated that 'the arches supporting the walled terrace were probably cloisters connecting it with the chapel, which is at the back of the present house'. He went on to guess, 'It is not improbable that the present house and the garden walls were constructed from the remains of the old monastery.' Half-baked theories mingle with half-remembered history uttered in a party game of Chinese whispers – dissolute monks, dissolved monasteries; dissolving bath salts; Bishop Rudd's bath (or was the bath Roman?) in popular myth. Historians firmly quash this: had a monastery existed here, some documentary record of it would certainly have survived. Just the faintest echo of a medieval monkish connection lingers – between not Aberglasney specifically but the parish church of Llangathen and a Chester priory.[29]

The Roman rather than Romanesque associations inspired by Aberglasney's arched openings make more sense. Fragments and larger vestiges of buildings of classical Rome were the inspiration behind the architecture of the Renaissance in Italy. The garden-makers of sixteenth-century Italy developed the use of arcades and terracing to perfection, modulating the contours of sloping ground and also creating artificial changes of height by building garden enclosures incorporating airy walkways above shady colonnades. The spatial interplay of inside and outside, above and below was capable of infinite architectural permutation. It also made enjoyment of the gardens by the visitor infinitely variable (as it still does in gardens today): it is pleasant to choose to walk in sun or cool shade, to mount to the heights and look either outward at the surrounding gardens and countryside, or downward and inward to the patterned gardens encompassed by the structures, or to seek cloistered seclusion. Arches provided shelter for tender plants, settings for statuary or cool, introspective retreats for living human figures, while airy summer houses and pavilions offered shelter of a different, lighter kind. Classical models survived for some of the structures adopted in the new Italian gardens of the Renaissance. Hadrian's Villa, for instance, contained a standing example of the covered walkway open on one side that was known by the splendid name of cryptoporticus, and of which the western side of the courtyard at Aberglasney is a form. But 'The happenstance of Roman topology also engineered garden ideas and forms that were originally totally unconnected with antique gardens: thus the half-buried arches of *thermae*, or baths, sometimes with modern "gardens" in front of them, provided arcades and terracing.'[30] Some echo of the same thought perhaps influenced sceptics who saw the Courtyard Garden at Aberglasney at its nadir. The arches at Aberglasney too were half-buried before the restoration process got under way. At the height of the infestation by weeds and rampant undergrowth it was hard to envisage their true dimensions, let alone to believe that they could have been purpose-built as an ornamental feature. The faithful, or hopeful, however, barely wavered in this conviction. Possible connections, sources of inspiration, parallels were eagerly sought out by the experts.

One hare that was raised led to Italy. Similarities between a word-picture of Aberglasney and one of the Villa Imperiale near Pesaro became exciting when it was found that the first description in English was that of one William Thomas, a Welshman, in his *History of Italy* first published in the reign of Edward VI. Was he related to our William Thomases? Had this work or the villa somehow inspired Aberglasney? Were there any links? This hare was knocked on the head when the Thomases were found to be 'no relation', as they say in *Private Eye*, and however hard people tried to find a direct connection, none could be found. In the end, one of the earliest wild guesses, hazarded when Aberglasney's restoration was no more than a dream, came closest to pinpointing, if not any direct inspiration, at least the correct historical period.

The description that resounds with echoes of Aberglasney comes from the essay 'Upon the Gardens of Epicurus' (1685), where Sir William Temple recalled a garden he had known thirty years earlier.[31] Like Aberglasney, it lay on a hillside that was not too steep. From a broad terrace in front of the house one might descend via one of three flights of steps into a compartmented parterre garden with an arcade on either side, or one could walk from the terrace along the top of those two arcades and look down into the garden and outward in the opposite directions across open country. Temple's description indicated that there was a summer house at each corner:

The steps uncovered

RIGHT AND BELOW LEFT *Phil Evans and Richard Scott-Jones at work at parapet walkway level. By clearing away soil and plant debris they were able to uncover traces of the upper flight of steps that led directly to the raised walkway from an intermediate platform or landing.*

They also established how the walkway was surfaced in the past, with a seal of puddled clay covered with a layer of chippings and finished with fine gravel.

RIGHT *An intermediate stage of the excavation of the steps shows how traces of the steps within the wall had been masked by the later blocking (in left* *of picture) which brought the inner face of the courtyard into alignment. The landing where the steps change direction is clearly emerging in the centre*

A new phase of archaeology began inside the Cloister Garden and revealed the ramp to be a Victorian 'modernization'.

ABOVE With the stonework cleaned up it becomes easy to 'read' the triangular scar on the face of the inner wall. Twin flights of steps ran up to meet at a central platform and then turned left in a single flight to reach the walkway level. That slope at the back is a Victorian red herring.

the sides of the parterre are ranged with two large cloisters, open to the garden, upon arches of stone, and ending with two other summer-houses even with the cloisters, which are paved with stone, and designed for walks of shade, there being none other in the whole parterre. Over these two cloisters are two terrasses covered with lead, and fenced with balusters; and the passage into these airy walks is out of the two summer-houses, at the end of the first terras-walk.

Was Aberglasney's cloistered walkway ever crowned with summer houses? None is mentioned in the following account of the 'small but remarkable old piece of gardening' that one later writer found in a 'moderately large quadrangle' beside the house at Aberglasney:

On three sides of the quadrangle there is a kind of covered walk, under a stone roof, supported by stone columns, with a stone balustrade above. . .a second broad walk, with garden beds as borders, is carried over the walk below, so that persons from the trim garden above can look down on to the trim garden with its cool water and fountain below.

The *Gardeners Chronicle* correspondent of 1892 was convinced that this was a relic of the Stuart period: 'It requires but little effort on the part of a wanderer in this charming garden of old times to people the place once more with the gentlemen and pretty ladies of Jacobean times.' But then, this was written at the height of the Victorian fashion for revivalism, when historical images were in everyone's mind. Ancient-looking structures were bang up-to-date, and conversely new designs aspired to an antique pedigree.

The Aberglasney-like garden layout that Sir William Temple described was indeed a Jacobean one. It was at Moor Park in Hertfordshire, created by Lucy Harington in the decade between 1617 and 1627. Temple spent his honeymoon there and remembered it through rose-tinted memory as 'the sweetest place, I think, that I have ever seen in my life, either before or since, at home or abroad'. Nothing now remains of the garden at Moor Park, and attempts to visualize it are dependent on Temple's eloquent work-picture, and on Roy Strong's sketch of a reconstruction.[32] However, with the exception of the summer houses, garden visitors of today in search of the 'airy walks' or 'walks of shade' typical of lost gardens like Moor Park might well find a replica of the experience by exploring the parapet walks and cool arcades of Aberglasney's Cloister Garden.

Aberglasney, February 1999. The Cloister Garden is once again the focus of a party. No music, no dancing this time: or at least only the lively toing and froing, wheeling and circling of keen minds engaging in stirring intellectual debate. The Aberglasney Restoration Trust has brought together a distinguished gathering of professional people who have been deeply involved in aspects of the restoration with experts from the outside world; together they are to consider all the evidence accumulated so far and hammer out what we know of the origins of the Cloister Garden. A brainstorming barn dance. The ABC detail of those invited includes – besides members and staff of the Trust itself (and the BBC film crew who record all aspects of the restoration) – Kevin Blockley, archaeologist; Sabine Eiche, expert in the gardens of Renaissance Italy; Craig Hamilton, architect for the building firm of Capps and Capps who are involved in rebuilding the garden structures; Paula Henderson, historian of Tudor and Stuart gardens; Penelope Hobhouse, designer of the new layout for the Upper Walled Garden and also an authority on period gardens; Mike Ibbotson, representing the landscape architects Colvin and Moggridge; Tom Lloyd, author of *The Lost Houses of Wales* and authority on historic buildings and local history and Andrew Sclater, the landscape consultant who was involved in the early stages of appraising the prospects of restoring Aberglasney.

We listen first to Kevin Blockley's summary of the results of recent archaeology in the Cloister Garden and elsewhere. Miraculously the western range of the structures – the Cloister walkway itself – can be dated quite precisely to around 1600. The two side ranges, formerly thought to be contemporaneous, turn out to be slightly newer – maybe a generation or so later. (That is, they do so in the arcaded form we see today, leading towards the house: plain stone walls might once have followed the print of their outer margins, and it is also possible that at an intermediate stage there was a return at either end of the cloister range with a staircase of some design to allow access to the parapet walkway.) We learn that there had been previous buildings and structures on the site, but their traces show them to be on a different alignment, at an angle to that of today. The roughly rectilinear present-day relationship of house, courtyard, Pool Garden – and gatehouse-plus-yew-tunnel complex – suggested that the whole surviving ground plan was likely the result of a single, though not necessarily continuous, phase of conception – say, sometime in the latter half of the Tudor period. (The fact that it is still not possible to locate the exact footprint of the early house hardly affects this current diagnosis.)

The relatively precise archaeological dating sets bells ringing in different registers. In the specific instance of Aberglasney we know that the half-century between 1590 and 1640 was a period of prosperity. We don't know exactly when Bishop Rudd came on the scene. (He was buying other properties hereabouts by the early 1600s – before or after acquiring the Big House in Llangathen? His wealthy, worldly predecessor Sir William Thomas put the date stone 'W.T./G. 1606' on Coed Helen, his new house, so it is confirmed that he and his wife Gaenor were well away in North Wales by then.) We do know that the bishop's son Sir Rice Rudd was a rising star in the firmament of the Court of King James – just the sort of milieu in which upwardly mobile country gentlemen with ambitious garden-making schemes might exchange fashionable ideas.

At the heart of an enigma

Here the garden historians step forward (in our recent Aberglasney party) to compare notes on how the strange structures at Aberglasney generally shape up to being accorded genuine Tudor/Stuart pedigrees. Their lack of precise geometry and symmetry is, perhaps surprisingly, unsurprising. A vista from the house through the cloister range to the pool would not necessarily be based on the concept of a central axis, we learn: the view from the side of the present house along the northern range would suffice. The geometry of juxtaposed rectangular enclosures would have emerged from the chemistry of the site – crystallized – without a predetermined overall plan (that came with Palladio as a later concept), like the series of quadrangles in an Oxbridge college – an organic growth. And the fact that the building quality is simply not very good ('farmyard architecture', said someone) reflects the fact that gardens and buildings at the time were generally not architect-planned to a blueprint but *constructed*, from an idea of the owner and/or his representative together with the art of the master-mason on the spot.

ABOVE LEFT
Archaeologist Kevin Blockley points out dramatic discoveries where the north-east end of the parapet walk descends to ground level near the corner of the house. The sloping ramp proved to be a Victorian adaptation of a much earlier and more elaborate formal design involving a double set of steps.

Perhaps built from some flawed pattern or not entirely familiar idea, it is possible to understand why the building blocks at Aberglasney are somewhat imperfect. Sources of inspiration for progressive, cultured house-making landowners were flooding into Britain by this time. Images of Italian Renaissance gardens again shimmer into consideration. Could one of our Aberglasney builders have been to Italy, read William Thomas, seen drawings, explored gardens where slopes were moulded by theatrical feats of terracing – or even heard about using archways and niches to display statues or to protect tender plants? The party came up with no answers. No direct link has been found. But then again, we do not know for certain that there was none.

Aberglasney keeps many of its mysteries. As we enjoy the walks and views, the light and shade of the Cloister Garden we tread in the steps of the Stuarts. We are in a Jacobean garden. We still don't know who built it, or quite why. But, thanks to archaeology, we do now know when.

RIGHT *A close look at such detail suggests the presence of some garden building here dating perhaps from no later than the Stuart era. A wider view of the context brought the exciting realization that the mysterious 'room' is on alignment with the medieval gatehouse tower seen beyond the wall.*

ABOVE *This area clearly needed further investigation. A preliminary trench revealed the presence of some kind of paved floor.*

RIGHT *The paving proved to be a highly decorative infill of pitched pebbles within a diaper pattern of larger stones. It appeared to be the flooring of a little room or pavilion, a theory endorsed by the discovery of fine-grade mortar on the adjacent inner walls.*

Trenching the formal garden: early work

LEFT AND BELOW *The Welsh Historic Gardens Trust commissioned Lesley Howes to do a preliminary assessment in 1992. Local WHGT volunteers dug a trench in the south-west corner of the garden and uncovered the paved flooring of the cloister itself. Landscape consultant Andrew Sclater (in striped jumper) directs operations.*

RIGHT *In 1995 Dyfed Archaeological Trust Field Operations undertook a second-phase evaluation of the garden. A trench dug westwards from the bay window uncovered only functional drains near the house, but in the centre of the area revealed the brick and mortar foundation of a circular fountain, the focal point of the Victorian layout. It was later filled with topsoil and turned into a flower bed.*

The 1990s saw several phases of archaeology in the Cloister Garden – in 1992, 1995 and 1998–9. The ground level had risen considerably over the last century, so even Victorian features were hidden. Somewhere even deeper must lie the ground plan that was contemporaneous with the cloisters themselves.

RIGHT *The structures brought to light by the 1995 trench corroborated a Gardeners Chronicle article of 1892 describing the 'moderately large quadrangle' beside the house in which 'a large stone-bordered pool of water has been formed, with a fountain, aquatic plants, and gold fish in the centre'.*

69

ABOVE *Cambrian Archaeological Projects' dig in the summer of 1998 was a more exhaustive affair. A large trench was cut through the length of the garden from house to cloisters in an attempt to find what the original levels had been, and whether the ground was graded in a slope or stepped into terraces.*

LEFT *Near the house archaeologists found evidence of a retaining wall, indicating that the building had once sat on a broad well-proportioned terrace. Beneath it the ground sloped gently away to another retaining wall parallel to the cloisters, although the stones of this had been robbed out at some earlier stage.*

Trenching the Formal Garden: in-depth investigations

ABOVE *The narrow opening in the angle of the north range is an oddity, and must have been remodelled several times. Stonework found in front of it proved to be part of a flight of steps leading into the corner. It's possible this was once part of a single-arched extension at either end of the original cloister range.*

LEFT *At one stage the three sides of the Cloister Garden were thought to date from the same building phase, but it emerged that construction of the western arcade predated the main side ranges by twenty or thirty years. These may have been simple outer walls at first, rather than the complex structures we see today.*

RIGHT *The arched gateway near the western end of the north range gives an oblique view from the Cloisters. Immediately beyond this gateway, to the right but unseen, is the building now known as the Gardener's Cottage. Beneath this area are traces of much older structures on a different alignment.*

BELOW *Whatever their original purpose, the apertures in the garden have had various uses in more recent centuries. The archway facing as you look along the western cloister range had at some time been blocked up leaving a small doorway. The resulting room could be reached from inside the cloisters. A storeroom perhaps? Or, as legend has it, the room where poachers were detained?*

ABOVE *An aerial view of the 1995 excavations in the north-west corner shows some cobbling.*

Also visible are modern waste pipes, a reminder that there have been generations of disturbance here.

Trenching the Formal Garden: the Cloister passage

LEFT *In 1998 the team from Cambrian Archaeological Projects cleared the wide cobbled path alongside the cloister range. The path was formerly bordered on the garden side by a terrace wall, its presence now indicated only by a robber trench made when the stones were dismantled for use elsewhere. (The man on the left with a spade is working on this trench.)*

RIGHT *The north-west corner (with its hint of steps leading into a passageway) provided evidence of later alterations. What looked like a squared-off planting bed contained a rich deposit of domestic refuse datable to the early 1700s.*

LEFT *Achaeologist Phil Evans is seen stepping around the stones of the newly uncovered wall, built across the cobbled surface sometime in the early eighteenth century, perhaps to make a planting bed.*

CHAPTER THREE

Reflections of the Past

The Pool Garden and
the Dyer Dynasty

A SUNLESS, STILL, LIFELESS DAY between winter and spring. Aberglasney's pool lies dreary below the brooding walls. Someone whispered: 'It's Mariana's Moated Grange!' For decades in the twentieth century Aberglasney remained neglected, its flower-plots and vegetable beds thickly encrusted with 'blackest moss' while (as in Tennyson's poem) rusted nails fell from the knots that pinned fruit-trees to the walls and doors creaked upon their hinges.

> About a stone-cast from the wall
> A sluice with blackened waters slept,
> And o'er it many, round and small,
> The clustered marish-mosses crept. . .

For years no saviour was in sight. A couple of knights errant in the guise of hopeful owners tried to take things in hand after the Evans family sold the property in the early 1950s, but to little avail. It took the Aberglasney Restoration Trust to ride in on its shining white charger and humming yellow machinery to mount a rescue.

The Pool Garden, which we encounter below the Cloister Garden, suffered particularly badly in the interregnum. Wall cappings crumbled as ivy plunged its roots ever deeper into the soft mortar. The long range of the Victorian vinehouse along the north side cracked, collapsed and disappeared, leaving only its naked rear wall. Centenarian conifers outgrew their strength and sickened, or indeed thrived out of all proportion. The level in the pool itself grew ever lower due to damage to its clay lining. And at the same time the water depth was being reduced by silt – and perhaps by jetsam. Aberglasney's pool has always been prone to the build-up of sediment. In living memory it has been dredged several times, and a bill of 1803 exists for draining, cleaning and repairing the fishpond. No doubt unrecorded operations of this kind were carried out in the intervals.

Meanwhile its surface was increasingly scummed by weed and algae, more reminiscent of the 'sluice' in Tennyson's poem than of its proper role as pool or fishpond. It was very different too from the clear water implied in John Dyer's poem 'The Country Walk', written in praise of 'the poet's pride, the poet's home', with its allusion to Aberglasney's 'gloomy bowers and shining lakes'. That plural – lakes – is probably poetic licence, as is the exaggeration of the size: Aberglasney's pool at its most

The water level is high and the surface is clear, mirror-like, reflecting the sky – ruffled only where newly contoured inlets spout water from a rill to refresh the great still body of the pool.

brimming hardly amounts to a lake, and it was probably smaller in John Dyer's day. But it almost certainly existed then, in the first quarter of the eighteenth century. It feels as if it must have been there as long as there have been dwellings and gardens on the site. The bank that holds the water is manmade, and the pool itself must have been deepened and excavated, but its site in a low basin before the ground slopes down and away is an inherently logical point for water to collect. (There is always plenty of water to collect at Aberglasney: this is wet West Wales. Garden designers can often get away with truly natural water features, with only minimal use of artificial devices for pumping and recycling.) And the Pool Garden's openness, enhanced by its reflections of the sky, seems an essential complement to the enclosed confines of the cloisters.

Let's look at what a garden pool might have meant to Aberglasney's incumbents over the centuries. First its role would have been utilitarian, as a place to breed or stock prized freshwater fish, although surely the magnetic attraction of water would have brought a measure of enjoyment to anyone strolling in the gardens. Later it would be valued primarily for its aesthetic attractions, although gardeners, waterfowl and who knows what amphibious creatures would have made use of it. Generations of visiting herons from the nearby heronry will have mutely witnessed all these episodes – when they were not themselves being hunted.

Lewis Glyn Cothi made no specific mention of water in his poetic description of Rhydderch's nine gardens, but if there was a medieval house of substance here it would have had its fishpond and stewponds. 'Fishponds were medieval status symbols, and their produce was reserved strictly for special feasts and the arrival of important guests.'[1] The presence of the pool lent credence to the supposition that Aberglasney had monastic origins, an idea that persisted for most of the twentieth century. 'Aberglasney had been a monastic foundation,' asserted Ralph Williams in his 1956 biography of John Dyer. Fifty years before that, in the early 1900s, Colonel Mayhew held forth his theories to this effect to a visiting party of antiquarians: 'The fishpond, which still contains carp and eels, was probably in existence when the monks resided here. If, from the disturbed state of the country, they were unable to go as far as the river to obtain fish for Fridays and their fast days, they were quite certain of a supply close at hand.'[2]

Not only does doubt hang over the existence of any religious foundation at Aberglasney; the very supposition that monks and fishponds were inevitably linked

ABOVE *Robert Dyer, the second of that name to own Aberglasney, was the elder brother of the poet John. In about 1720 he inherited the estate from his father and married Frances Croft. This portrait is said to be by John Dyer, more famous for poems like 'Grongar Hill' than as a painter.*

turns out to be something of a red herring. It appears that long before the monasteries embarked on creating fishponds, prosperous secular households had them as a matter of course.[3] This means that from the time of Elystan Glodrydd (the first name on our family tree) a fish-stocked pool would have been a likely ingredient of the well-appointed residence. Only in about 1200 did the monasteries too begin to build fishponds and stewponds on any scale, as if to keep up with the Joneses of the time.

Then about a hundred years later we have Llywelyn ap Llywelyn Ddu, who was surnamed Foethus (the Luxurious). Many newcomers to Aberglasney have noted this strange title and wondered what it implies – in what sphere of indulgence did 'Black' Llywelyn's son earn that name? Let us for the moment assume that it refers to the splendour of his home and the sumptuousness of his board. What would Aberglasney's fishpond have meant to the wealthy, self-indulgent landowner at the turn of the fourteenth century?

Let's consult the heron of the day as oracle. Today its descendants are politely discouraged by most pond-owners because of the depradations a heron can make on fish stocks. The earlier landowner might have been more ambivalent, because – although they might take steps to scare one away from robbing their fishpond – members of the medieval gentry were keen to establish heronries for sport. Owen Glendower was an example: 'A heronry, which was a concomitant of the seat of every great man, supplied him and his guests with game for the sport of falconry.'[4] Large birds like herons were hunted with peregrine falcons; as luxuries for the table they were larded, roasted and eaten with ginger.[5]

Sport of a more modern kind took its toll on Aberglasney's local heronry in the 1960s when pigeon-shooting took place in the wood where the herons nested. That generation of herons all decamped to Allt-y-Gaer. Our token heron seeks to make another point. It reminds us that owners of heronries in Wales have sometimes believed that their family would die out if the heronry ceased to be occupied.[6] Given Aberglasney's history in the last four centuries, when several human lines have petered out, the habits of the contemporaneous herons might well deserve monitoring.

All this might have meant that meatless days ordained first by the Church and then by secular law, and affecting not just religious institutions but all good, law-abiding Christian households, were not inevitably miserable. The hospitality that visitors and itinerant bards like Lewis Glyn Cothi received from their host is bound to have included delicious feasts of fish. Even after the Reformation Sir William Thomas and his family would still find fish on the table at a high proportion of their meals – its source now (if not the Towy) as often the sea as the fishpond. With meat animals scarce and Spanish seapower threatening, Elizabeth I found it pragmatic to boost fish consumption so as to encourage the useful skills of boatbuilding and sailing, fishermen being 'the chiefest nurse for mariners of this land'. In 1594, the year Anthony Rudd became Bishop of St David's, Queen Elizabeth passed laws to make Fridays and Saturdays 'fish days', and further proclamations against eating meat in Lent and on other fasting days were made during the reign of James I.

With the end of compulsory fish days after the Restoration, freshwater fish generally went out of favour in the diet of those able to choose what they ate. River fish would be preferred to still-water kinds. And one of Aberglasney's Dyer residents evinced an almost unhealthy passion for fishing, if not for fish-eating, as we find from his Commonplace book quoted later on. For a time some of the gentry kept their fishponds as reservoirs of freshwater fish. But during the eighteenth century most landowners allowed their pools and lakes to lapse into ornamental waters, remodelling them as landscape features.

The eighteenth-century landowners at Aberglasney were the Dyers. (We are now embarking on this chapter's history module.) The house was purchased with other property in 1710 by Robert Dyer from the Hon. Thomas Watson-Wentworth, of Wentworth Woodhouse in Yorkshire, who held a mortgage on the estate of the financially embarrassed Rudds, whose plight we recorded in the last chapter. The dry account of the official chroniclers contradicts a popular version, which has bullets flying and a right old commotion attending the transfer of the property – one of the moments of high drama that occasionally enliven this usually peaceful scene. It is possible that the Dyers were already living at Aberglasney as tenants before completing the purchase: one of John Dyer's biographers cites the 'amusing legend. . .of the unwillingness of the previous occupants to give up Aberglasney to the Dyers, who lived there for some years as tenants before purchasing it in 1710'[7]:

Aberglasney is said to have been purchased by [John] Dyer's father, Robert, a successful solicitor, under a decree of the Court of Chancery, on the insolvency of

ABOVE *Frances was one of the three daughters of Sir Herbert Croft of Croft Castle in Herefordshire. An eighteenth-century authority attributed the head to Sir Godfrey Kneller and said of the sitter: 'This beautiful woman was very flighty, almost insane.' Today's experts think the painter was probably John Dyer.*

Sir Rice Rudd after a severely contested election, and on terms so favourable to the purchaser that he resold detached farms for prices sufficient to pay for the whole estate. An old tenant who died aged 85, told the late owner, Mr Walters Philipps, that his grandfather had witnessed a bloody contest between the Rudd and Dyer parties about possession, Dyer bringing in a strong force of strangers and ultimately succeeding.[8]

This account of the 1870s records the links in the chain through which the tradition was handed down over more than a century and a half. 'Much of this story is true, in spite of the omission of Sir Thomas Watson-Wentworth as an intervening owner between Sir Rice Rudd, Bart., and Robert Dyer; the battle could have occurred when the Dyers sought to take possession as tenants of Sir Thomas,' the biographer surmises; we could add that the intervening Sir Anthony Rudd might have put his oar in, since in 1705 we find him instituting an action in the High Court of Chancery against Storey Barker, Watson-Wentworth and others in an attempt to recover possession of his inheritance.

If the Dyer family lived as tenants at Aberglasney it seems unlikely that they did so before 1703, since their child born in that year was baptized in Llanfynydd rather than in Llangathen.

What seems certain is that once the purchase was completed Robert Dyer rebuilt at least part of the house and finally moved in with his family – four sons survived – in 1714, although rebuilding of some kind was still taking place at his death in 1720. The work must have been well under way in 1717. In May that year Sir Erasmus Philipps of Picton Castle was passing through the Towy valley on one of his self-improving tours and remarked on its more noteworthy properties, including Golden Grove and Abermarlais. Upriver from Abergwili, he passed 'Broad Oak – on the right in a pleasant Grove lies Aberglasney the beautiful seat of Robt Dier Esq.'[9] Garden enthusiasts will be interested to note his reference to the surrounding 'grove'. One definitive achievement of this construction phase was the redesigned front façade with its up-to-the-minute symmetry, as we saw in Chapter One. With the limewash of soft umber (an unexpected piece of evidence revealed only by the removal of the portico), the house must have gleamed in the green landscape like sunlight on ripening barley, a fine advertisement for the taste of its new owners.

We can only speculate about what other changes Robert Dyer saw fit to make to the dwelling and the gardens that the Rudd family had left. Did he merely 'put a new face on it'? Someone ambitious enough to order the redesigning of his house in the very latest style is likely to have wanted other improvements besides the cosmetic one of the new façade. A note from his son John makes the sweeping statement that he 'rebuilt it'. But what does that mean? What had the Dyers in mind in acquiring Aberglasney?

If the Church had been the Rudds' springboard to ownership, it was the law that enabled the Dyer family to enter the ranks of the landed gentry. The Dyers were townsfolk and tradesmen who emerged in the fifteenth and sixteenth centuries as burgesses in first Carmarthen and then Kidwelly. Aberglasney's Robert Dyer was the son of another Robert (baptized in Kidwelly in 1634) and his wife Mary, of whom little is known – although John Dyer's note on his ancestry will give a clue. Robert Dyer the lawyer and his wife Catherine (*née* Cocks) left Kidwelly and moved to an unidentified house in the parish of Llanfynydd.[10] Here six or perhaps seven children were born and baptized between 1695 and 1703, of whom four sons grew to adulthood.

The parish church of Llanfynydd is in the village, nearly four miles to the north of Aberglasney as the crow flies: a significant distinction, for they are a long, twisting four miles by road, precisely the sort of forbidding terrain that impressed visitors with the inhospitable nature of vast tracts of Wales. It made the cosmopolitan contrast of Carmarthen and the luxuriant Towy valley all the more attractive. In his *Tour Through the Whole Island of Great Britain* (1724–7) Daniel Defoe described Carmarthen in the Dyers' time as 'well Built, and Populous' and 'found the People of this County more civiliz'd, and more curteous, than in the more Mountainous Parts, where the Disposition of the Inhabitants seems to be rough, like the Country: But here they seem to Converse with the rest of the World, by their Commerce, so they are more conversible than their Neighbours.' Robert Dyer's practice at law was in the prosperous town of Carmarthen. He was himself sufficiently prosperous to invest in land. He purchased the manor of the Priory of Kidwelly, properties in Llangathen and nearby parishes, and, in 1710, the mansion house of Aberglasney.

Robert Dyer appears to have been a cut above the everyday provincial lawyer, both in ability and connections, high and perhaps low. A generation after his death he was remembered by his son John's biographers as 'an attorney of great practice and reputation' and 'a solicitor of great capacity and note': descriptions more notable for their efficiency than their humanity. He ran a decidedly tight ship, although his professional practice seems to have been no worse than that of most of his contemporaries: action in the courts moved slowly in the eighteenth century, and lawyers made the most of every opportunity to charge heavily in the matter of expenses. Robert Dyer seems to have been adept both at holding back funds from his clients, and at overcharging them.[11]

He was also remarkably well connected. We simply do not know how it came about that he acted as agent for some of the most substantial landowners in the area. The schedule of debts chargeable to Robert Dyer's personal estate includes the names of the sixth Duke of Somerset, the Bishop of St David's, the Marquis of Powis, the Marquis of Carmarthen and John Eyre, Esq.[12] When we consider his architectural ambition in rebuilding the front façade of Aberglasney, we might remember that the Rudds' mortgagee from whom he purchased Aberglasney was Thomas Watson-Wentworth, whose son was about to embark on the building of the ostentatiously vast

RIGHT AND BELOW
The pool was barely visible beneath the vegetation that had colonized the deep silt. The first task was to clear this invasive vegetation and to locate and repair the pool's damaged retaining stone wall.

BELOW *After the hardcore was spread, fresh clay was brought in to be compacted by heavy machinery into a watertight seal.*

LEFT *With the pool drained, work began on making good the puddled clay lining. A layer of hardcore was spread over the most badly damaged areas of the pool.*

Early work on the Pool Garden: structural repairs

ABOVE *The cleared pond holds water once again, reflecting the sky and its surroundings. The presence of the island has prompted controversy – is it an ugly intrusion in the calm expanse of water, or does it serve as an eyecatcher when glimpsed from within the Cloister Garden?*

Aberglasney's pool has always had a tendency to silt up. Records from the nineteenth and twentieth centuries show that periodically it has had to be drained and cleared.

LEFT *The pool surrounds, cleared for action and staked out for surveying. The diseased cryptomeria near Gardener's Cottage is doomed to be felled, but the lonesome pine whose shadow leads us into the picture will remain as part of a new planting scheme.*

RIGHT *Gardener Michael Thurlow in glyphosate gear, standing in the no-man's-land west of the Pool Garden and near the gardeners' yard. Repeated applications of* *weedkiller can eventually suppress the dreaded Japanese knotweed, but vigilance is needed to spot newly sprouted root fragments and deal with them in good time.*

Surveying the pool surrounds

ABOVE The Pool Garden from the south-east corner, with Gardener's Cottage to the right. The blank far wall (with farm buildings behind) once supported a magnificent vine-house. The taped area in the foreground signals investigation around the water outfall into the pond.

new house of Wentworth Woodhouse in Yorkshire, with its façade of unprecedented length. But Robert Dyer perhaps had his thugs and wide boys too: in the fracas over his taking possession of his property from the reluctant Rudds, he is supposed to have engaged the support of that 'strong force of strangers'.

It seems that Robert Dyer's eminent business connections provided him with inspiration and models to emulate. These made him concerned to establish the Dyers as a 'county family' – witness his interest in genealogy and his desire to build up a large property in Carmarthenshire. It is ironic that we remember the Robert Dyer who bought Aberglasney not for any of this, but because his memory is preserved through the reputation of one of his sons in a sphere of which the lawyer entirely disapproved.

Two of Robert Dyer's sons are of particular interest to the story of Aberglasney: Robert, the oldest surviving son, who became the heir to Aberglasney and so physically owned and occupied the property with which we are concerned, and John, a year younger, the poet who made Aberglasney famous. A first son, also baptized John, did not survive infancy.

Progress in the Pool Garden

ABOVE, RIGHT *Two views from the west, with 'before and after' messages and a slightly shifted viewpoint. The archway between Pool and Cloister Gardens is a common factor in the far wall.*

Progress in the pool surround (above), with hardcore paths laid for the benefit of a different kind of plant – bulldozers, diggers and dumpers that will colonize the garden for a season or two. Later things will change as levels around the pool are investigated and found to have been much lower in the past. Excess topsoil, rich with silt from earlier pond-clearings, will go to improve the Upper Walled Garden.

ABOVE *The same view taken from further back. Winter has stripped the weeping ash of foliage but it is hard work by human hands that has denuded the Cloister Garden wall of its shrouding vegetation and restored it to almost shocking starkness. The ash was already mature in a photograph taken around 1870, which also showed glasshouses at the spot where this picture was taken.*

LEFT *The pool is glimpsed through an unrestored scooped crenellation on the parapet. These shapes are blurred by ivy in arborescent mode – its clinging stems can climb no further upwards, so assume a tree-like habit and begin to flower.*

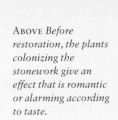

ABOVE *Before restoration, the plants colonizing the stonework give an effect that is romantic or alarming according to taste.*

ABOVE *The repaired wall depends on tree shadows to mask its nakedness. From its profile archaeologists think the opening may have been built some time after the wall itself was completed.*

The main archway: entrance to Cloister and Pool

ABOVE AND LEFT
Through the main archway in two directions: from poolside towards house (above), the archway unrestored; and from Cloisters towards pool (left). It forms a vital link between the two enclosures, yet garden historians feel its central position is not authentic to a Jacobean layout.

87

We are indebted to an autobiographical fragment of the poet's for information that seems to have been overlooked by some earlier chroniclers of Aberglasney under the Dyers. Like so many papers relating to Aberglasney the original has been lost – someone in the 1920s took it upon themselves to destroy John Dyer's letters to his brother Thomas in the belief that no one in the twentieth century could possibly be interested in this long-dead poet – but this surviving snippet was transcribed by a more enlightened nineteenth-century descendant. It seems that the family were not simply *arrivistes* from outside investing in a promising piece of real estate but had strong connections with the area, and indeed with Aberglasney itself. John Dyer wrote:

> My great grandfather had an estate in Llandilo parish called Kaglassran but sold that and bought Abersannen in Lanvynwith [Llanfynydd] parish of Sir Rice Rudd of Aberglasney. His wife was of the Hicks, an ancient family in Kidwelly, descended from the Gowers.
>
> My grandmother was the daughter of Williams Esqr. of Brinhavod in the parish of Llangathen, descended from Sir William Thomas of Aberglasney, who sold that house and estate to Bishop Rudd; 'twas then called Place-Llangathen. My father repurchased that seat and rebuilt it and was about completing it, but died. . .[13]

Here is John Dyer, poet, painter and eighteenth-century man of the world, participating for a brief moment in the Welsh genealogies game that we came across so frequently in Chapter One – where everyone is the son of X who is the son of Y and so on. He too could trace his ancestors in the area, by name and by dwelling-place. (We should perhaps note that the Sir Rice that Dyer mentions would have been the first baronet.) The places mentioned help to fill in some of the gaps in the Dyers' line of descent – that one grandmother of John Dyer and his siblings was Mary Williams of Brynhafod seems no longer in doubt.[14] Moreover, she was descended from our old friend Sir William Thomas of Aberglasney. Some of the Dyer forebears had actually lived at Aberglasney – the family belonged here. 'Sir William Thomas of Aberglasney. . .sold that house and estate to Bishop Rudd,' declares Dyer. In the continuing absence of any hard evidence for this precise transaction do we (or the more cynical among us) dismiss the statement as mere family myth and folklore? Or might we take John Dyer's word for it? A useful aside is his assertion that the estate was 'then called Place-Llangathen', that is, Plas Llangathen, with the implication that it was among the major houses of the parish. At last we have a handle on what people called the mansion before the name 'Aberglasney' came into circulation in the mid-sixteenth century. The farmstead of Abersannan, incidentally, is about as near to Aberglasney as you can get in Llanfynydd parish. Brynhafod, home of John's grandmother, is two miles due east of Abersannan and has a history of its own.[15] The three properties are less than an hour's walk apart.

John Dyer went to Westminster School and came back to Carmarthen to work in his father's office. Disliking legal work, he turned to the arts and became an adequate painter and an accomplished poet. But we shall return to this aspect of his life, and the light it sheds on Aberglasney, in our next chapter, when we consider the landscape that encompasses Aberglasney. Another brother, Thomas, went to Oxford and became a parson; the youngest son, Bennet (christened after the family of his maternal grandmother), married a neighbour's widow – Grace Lloyd of Berllandywyll – and moved to Cardiganshire, where he was High Sheriff in 1736. We might speculate whether it was to this lady that in the early 1730s her future brother-in-law the poet composed 'A Distich, To Mrs Llewdd of Berlandowil' that again touches on the native preoccupation with family trees:

Your old Welsh Pedigree is long you say – but pray consider this
　　Good Madam,
My Father, Father had, & he had his, & his, & his, & his,
　　To Adam.[16]

The oldest boy, Robert, is more central to the material fate of Aberglasney, and it is his story that we now follow. He was already reading law at Oxford by the time the family moved to the house at Aberglasney. He became a barrister at the Inner Temple and in about 1720, when he inherited Aberglasney on his father's death, married Frances, a daughter of Sir Herbert Croft, of Croft Castle, MP for Hereford and a descendant of Owen Glendower. (What might this tell us about the connections of this relatively modest Dyer family that made its name and reputation in the law?) Robert is an elusive character. He does not seem to have held public office or had a high profile in county affairs. Almost all we know of him is his reluctance in due course to pay his younger brothers the inheritance to which each was entitled under the terms of their father's will. He sounds a poor financial manager, and nor can he have inherited much of his father's flair for the law. His wife brought with her a fortune of £2000, but under the marriage agreement Robert transferred all his property to trustees, including lands intended for sale to raise ready money to pay off the legacies and debts of his father.[17]

Short of cash, with the rebuilding begun by his father to be completed and new prestigious family ties to keep up, the second Robert Dyer of Aberglasney took the estate into the 1720s and held the reins for thirty years. What changes he made during this time we simply do not know. Croft Castle, the Domesday-recorded ancestral home of his wife Frances, exercised no apparent influence.

Mr and Mrs Robert Dyer the second. We have a curious picture of the life of this couple and their children refracted through the eyes of Joseph Gulston, the celebrated collector of books and prints, who described a series of nine portraits he found hanging at Aberglasney when he visited in 1783. Among them was one of 'Mr Dyer, brother of the poet, down to the knees in a blue velvet coat, neckcloth twisted through the button hole.' His wife Frances Dyer was depicted 'sitting, a most beautiful woman. . .the head is painted by Sir Godfrey Kneller, but the neck, hand, and Drapery are bad, by some of his people'.[18] The prolific Kneller died in 1723: this must have been a late work. A more sinister note is struck by Gulston's suggestion of mental instability: 'This beautiful woman was very flightly, almost insane – the generation have suffered from this connexion.' Gulston perhaps had in mind a son, William, who was also affected: 'for many years before he became of age and till his death was out of his mind'.[19]

Two other sons were perfectly *compos mentis*, but this did not preserve them from life's vicissitudes, particularly financial ones. Both young men married daughters and co-heiresses of John Herbert, their near neighbour at Court Henry, a mile and a half to the west of Aberglasney. The younger, Francis Dyer, married Anna Maria Herbert in 1749 and settled in his wife's home. Robert Archer Dyer, who inherited the Aberglasney estates on his father's death in 1752, married Elizabeth Herbert in 1746. She brought with her a fortune of £1000.

The son Robert Archer Dyer was admitted to the Middle Temple in 1743. He is one of the handful of early characters to appear on the Aberglasney stage speaking his own lines, as it were, or at least in his own words. The youthful Robert Archer Dyer sounds full of good intentions, including one of immense value to the storyteller: it is 'to keep a Common Place Book'.[20] Through this document we hear fragments of the first person, and find – at last! – a few precious references to the gardens and grounds at Aberglasney, such as a list of his fruit trees – which we consider in Chapter Five. Jumbled in with these practicalities are notes of the self-improving, moralizing sort you would expect in such a worthy enterprise. In June 1745 he proposed:

> for the future that Husbandry shall take up the main of my thoughts, and to take
> a pleasure in walking over ye ground and observing what is wanted to be done,
> and to see what methods my tenants take to make up their rents, who is the best
> farmer, the most active and inductrious and most capable to improve the
> tenement, to censure ye lazy and unstriving tenant, and to encourage ye
> industrious one, and in general to search into ye customs, practices, and different
> methods of farming, that I may make up ye most of my estate.

As well as thus managing his estate astutely – perhaps in deliberate contrast to the example set by his father – he planned to improve himself with various reading schemes ('a very good method to sit every morning at your scrutore an hour to study your affairs') but there were lapses. The Dyers of Aberglasney perhaps took too eagerly to the pleasures of the role of country squire without equal attention to its responsibilities. A violent scarlet fever 'attended by a Quinzy' was a consequence of 'frequent taking of ye river in fishing ye months of April and May – 4 guineas to Dr Foy'. He resolved to learn from this experience: 'NB – I hope ye remembrance of this Distemper will check the too ardent desire of any sport whatsoever, as no sport, the most easy or gentle, if too violently pursued but will certainly hurt ye faculties of ye Body or mind in ye end.' But half a dozen years later Dr Foy was consulted again and warned that 'the distemper [was] brought on by fishing and a sedentary life,' a diagnosis in which Robert Archer Dyer could only concur.

Was Robert Archer Dyer unpractical or extravagant? He reproached himself for spending £47 6s. 10d. during a visit to London in 1743, resolving to allow himself '1s. 6d. *per diem, ne plus ultra*' from that moment. In 1746 we find him inscribing an 'Account of my cloaths – a green plush coat, silver buttons, a brown flowered silk waistcoat, a red knap waistcoat a brown fustian breeches, a red alapeen breeches, a black velvet breeches, two white Holland waistcoats, two white waistcoats with Jacks, two merry derry waistcoats. . .'. But then, this was the summer of his marriage.

Alliance with wealthy wives seemed no check to the downhill direction of the Dyer fortunes. In 1742 and again in 1743 Robert Dyer and his son Robert Archer Dyer mortgaged the Aberglasney estate in the sum of £1000 to Thomas Corbett of St Margaret's, Westminster. Shortly after his marriage Robert Archer Dyer mortgaged parts of his property in Llanegwad and Llangathen to his new father-in-law and later he sold off parts of his estate.

By 1768 he owed £2456 14s. 6d., which his elder son, William Herbert Dyer, undertook to discharge in due course. A tragedy of a different kind struck this year. His second son, Robert Herbert Dyer had become a midshipman in the Royal Navy. At ten o'clock on the night of 29 November 1768 he was walking on the deck of HMS *Boreas*, then lying off Lisbon, when 'a block fell on his head and kill'd him on ye spot'. He was just twenty. His brother officer, who witnessed the accident, wrote that he was 'decently interr'd at Lisbon'. Distraught and encumbered by debt, Robert Archer Dyer left Aberglasney and is found living in Bosbury, in Herefordshire, in 1770.

One fleeting glimpse of Robert Archer Dyer in the ensuing years is as puzzling as it is revealing. In about 1775 his name appears among the subscribers to the *Six Views in South Wales Drawn After Nature* produced by the underrated artist Thomas Jones of Pencerrig at that time. Perhaps he was an enthusiastic connoisseur, or nostalgic for Wales; perhaps family connections with Croft Castle were twisting his arm: at all events he was prepared to splash out on this series of prints.

After his father's retreat to Herefordshire, William Herbert Dyer (born in 1747) now did his best to weather the storms of debt that continued to batter the Aberglasney estate. He was a magistrate and served as High Sheriff of Carmarthenshire in 1776. At Aberglasney his fortunes fluctuated wildly. Early on he mortgaged the estate and incurred loans, then for a brief moment in 1785 managed to redeem the debts, but then three years later again mortgaged the estate for £2350 to Herbert Lloyd, an attorney of Carmarthen. Finally, in 1798, Willaim Herbert Dyer was obliged to instruct Herbert

The ivy problem

All the poetic romance of creeper-clad buildings has a grim counterpoint in the structural damage that can be caused by plants like ivy.

ABOVE AND RIGHT *Seedlings and climbers find a roothold in the soft mortar of untended buildings and loosen it still further. In the walls at Aberglasney whole sections of facing stone were prised away by invasive roots of woody plants. This revealed the poor quality of the original workmanship, with too few longer stones bonding the skin soundly into the rubble interior of the structures.*

Lloyd to advertise Aberglasney mansion and sixteen other properties in Llangathen parish for sale.

An estate agent's blurb is one thing. Before we take up the pinch of salt with which to swallow its blandishments, let's hear a description of the house by the connoisseur Joseph Gulston, whose assessment of the portraits of Robert and Frances Dyer we have already encountered. Gulston's viewpoint is an interesting one; indeed, he is a fascinating character. His parents' unconventional marriage engendered a bestselling nineteenth-century novel, and his own colourful life story is well worth seeking out. He became connected with Wales when he married the daughter of Sir Thomas Stepney, Baronet. Having studied the art collections held by royal palaces and great country seats like Blenheim and Marlborough, he unsurprisingly 'found, by comparison, the Welsh houses to be inferior, both in design and content, to their English counterparts'. His critical, unflattering approach can be taken as a reasonably accurate summary. He visited in 1783, and before listing the portraits in the house, made the following note:

> The seat of William Dyer, Esq, Carmarthenshire. An old house with a large Hall. In the centre is a Staircase which carry's you to a Chapel of which nothing now is remaining but the Pulpit which is old and curious. There is a terras round a court built on Stone Arches. It is close to Grongar Hill. The country is most beautiful.[21]

It is interesting that only seventy years after Robert Dyer the first was said to have 'rebuilt' it, Gulston is calling Aberglasney 'an old house'. The implication from this reliable witness is that a good deal remained of the older house built by the Rudds.

'The Mansion is Large and Handsome', ran the sweet, come-hither prose of Herbert Lloyd's 1798 advertisement. It consisted of 'four Good Rooms on the Ground Floor, with suitable bedrooms and convenient offices fit for the reception of a large Family, extensive outbuildings, a good Garden, and excellent Water at Command. . .'. The attractive Views were commended and the premises stated to be in good repair – which was not in fact the case. At first the asking price was £15,000; then it was dropped to 10,000 guineas. Now began an immensely protracted and convoluted series of negotiations, at the end of which the last of the Dyers of Aberglasney removed to London and then Shropshire, to die without issue in 1821, and Aberglasney came into the nineteenth century and the hands of Thomas Phillips.

The background to Thomas Phillips's acquisition of the property is the subject of Chapter Five. Here we'll concentrate on our saunter in the Pool Garden. This was the scene of considerable activity in the prelude to Surgeon Phillips's arrival from India, when a great deal of refurbishment was taking place in both house and estate. Accounts for 1803 allude to extensive work on the fishpond, which was drained, cleaned and repaired, and for which a new 'plug' was made. There is a theory that the pool was enlarged and made into a more regular shape around the middle decades of the nineteenth century. The Tithe Map of 1839 shows a broadly egg-shaped pool, its narrow end pointing just east of north; the Ordnance Survey map of 1888 shows the pool as the regular rectangle we see today. Does this represent a difference in mapping convention or a real change in the gardens?

If only the heron could tell us. It is possible that the pool did change shape over the years. Presented with an expanse of water, fashionable Stuart and early Georgian garden makers (the first Sir Rice Rudd, for instance, in the 1630s, or Robert Dyer around 1720) would surely have wanted to constrict it into an elongated shape, if not a coolly formal canal. Alternatively, a later Dyer might have devised a fidgety irregular shape to make the water feature look studiously natural, as when around the 1750s, the fictional character 'Squire Mushroom' adapted his farmhouse into a villa with a two-acre garden crammed with incident:

> At your first entrance, the eye is saluted with a yellow serpentine river, stagnating through a beautiful valley, which extends near twenty yards in length.[22]

Neither of these fashionable manifestations seems to have happened to our water feature. The regular shape of the pool was perfectly in accordance with what was *de rigueur* in the 1840s. The authoritative Jane Loudon (in a book that came out not long after Tennyson's 'Mariana' was published) proclaimed:

> Where ponds are intended solely for fish, without regard to their appearance in the landscape, their banks should be quite straight, and their shape square or oblong.[23]

An island or two 'for the swans and other aquatic birds to make their nests on' was desirable where the pond was of sufficient size – 'never less than five or six acres, and as much more as is convenient', which sounds unlike our Aberglasney fishpond; but our Aberglasney Victorians must have been happy that once again rectangular enclosures were good news, and it was fine to have a rectangular garden with a fishpond in it, as long as its banks were 'quite straight'. What did change during the later nineteenth century were the ground levels surrounding the pool. Original paths were found buried far below the surface of the garden that the Trust acquired. The new contours provided a narrow panel of slightly sloping ground between the long, blank outer wall of the Cloister Garden and the pool itself. This needed decorative treatment. A photograph of around 1900 shows this land as smooth lawn studded with predictable mirror-image symmetries of fashionable bedding plants. The three gardeners resting momentarily on their tools at the request of the photographer stare at us unfathomably.

We shouldn't forget another function of the garden pool – to stock an ice-house, *de rigueur* in the eighteenth and nineteenth centuries and definitely the sort of modern convenience that a wealthy owner like Thomas Phillips would want. Neighbours at Dynevor, Golden Grove and Middleton all had ice-houses, which still exist. Did Aberglasney have one? Where might it be? A sunless, north-facing slope was always preferred. We scrutinize the maps within a radius of a few hundred yards for possible sites. People are sometimes surprised at the distance of an ice-house from the kitchens. The governing factor seems not to be the inconvenience to the servants who must transport the blocks of ice to the kitchens, but the proximity of a pool to supply that initial stock of ice. The Tithe Map of 1839 shows a well-marked cart track from the 'wilderness' area through Pigeon House Wood heading southwest into a field of scrub before curving to end in an inscrutable symbol that could well represent the mounded earth above a subterranean ice-house. Strange that only forty years later there is no evidence of this track on the OS First Edition, generally so reliable for its accuracy in depicting tree type and so on. Perhaps the ice-house – if it was one – had fallen into disuse in the mid-nineteenth century. Perhaps the whole thing is another red herring – a new embellishment to the Aberglasney mythology.

The Pool Garden has other features beside the obvious one. To what date might we ascribe the creation of a vast span of glasshouses along the south-facing wall of the Pool Garden – a general improvement bringing Aberglasney up to date with advances in Victorian garden technology? This thoroughly practical, though ostentatious, modernizing step would form a garden counterpart to the purely cosmetic one of erecting a portico on the façade and probably dates from around the same time, when John Walters Philipps was in his heyday. It would be nice to discover an old photograph of the glasshouse, even in decay, to see if it provided any dating for this lost structure: the width of the glass panes, the method of ventilation, the general shape and style might enable the garden archaeologist to pinpoint the approximate date when it was put up, and thus add another piece to our jigsaw of the lives and expectations of our Aberglasney families. Some designs are readily recognizable among the advertisements that appeared in the burgeoning gardening periodicals of the nineteenth century. The structure is simply described in the *Tenby Observer* advertisement of 14 November 1872 as 'a Vinery, 40ft by 20ft'.

By Victoria's reign horticultural expertise had fine-tuned the art of growing dessert grapes. With hothouse technology you could defy the constraints of the climate. By choosing early or late varieties, by a combination of forcing premature fruiting and retarding ripening, and by artful storing strategies, a capable gardener could expect to provide grapes for the table in every month of the year. Our Aberglasney families from the Walters Philippses to the Mayhews might hope to impress their guests with succulent bloom-dusted grapes at all seasons. Perhaps they took the advice of Mrs

Beeton's *Book of Household Management* (1861) in making an arrangement of mixed fruit, with the 'Grapes. . .placed on the top of the fruit, a portion of some of the bunches hanging over the sides of the dish in a *négligé* kind of manner, which takes off the formal look of the dish'. Perhaps they also pondered on the qualities that made hygienists pronounce the grape as among the best of foods: 'it is nourishing and fattening, and its prolonged use has often overcome the most obstinate cause of constipation'. Grapes were almost certainly among the unspecified bounty sent at dead of winter to Pentypark, where Aberglasney's future heiress was staying with her uncle and aunt. 'After dinner we arranged flowers that came from Aberglasney and unpacked the fruit,' Mary Anne recorded in January 1868.[24]

In the garden when the Trust acquired Aberglasney not enough of the structure remained even to see whether the front wall of the vinery had arches at its feet: vine roots were often planted in the ground outside the house and the stems trained inside. Remnants of plumbing suggested that the heating system was based on hot pipes running through the glasshouse rather than by means of a hollow-flue wall: the half-subterranean boiler house still stands on the outside of the wall (and so outside the limits of the modern Aberglasney grounds). We might think of the generations of gardeners' boys who helped the head gardener perform all the finicky tasks that growing vines entailed – and who kept those boilers stoked on frosty nights to keep grapes and other exotics on the polished tables of the mansion. Perhaps they were grateful for a task that kept them warm.

For the new garden design consultant Hal Moggridge has planned a glorious 'hot border' planting for the bed that occupies the site of the old vine house. This is garden reincarnation, not restoration, and there was no question of Aberglasney Restoration Trust's rebuilding an authentic version of the lost structure, as has been done at places like West Dean in Sussex or Heligan in Cornwall. In terms of gardenworthiness this bed ranks high. It faces south, has a protecting wall behind it, and – being raised – probably has better drainage than some areas in this dampish climate. It is one of the most favoured places in the garden for growing Mediterranean-climate plants like *Erica arborea*, onopordum and *Convolvulus cneorum*. Hal Moggridge's rich colour theme uses silver and muted purple foliage with white, crimson and crimson-pink flowers, plus some dark evergreen leaves. His colleague Mike Ibbotson has designed a seat in an arbour partway along this border in the shelter of an ornamental purple-leaved vine. We should use words like claret and burgundy to describe the tones. I would like to think that as visitors rest in this shelter and glance upwards through vinous foliage made glowing by sunlight, they might feel some sense of communion with the vines that once grew here.

You could go back further, and remember the 'crooked vines' that Lewis Glyn Cothi praised as flourishing in Rhydderch ap Rhys's demesne. Was the poet again painting a somewhat rosy picture of his patron? Probably not: vineyards abounded in Britain from

Domesday to the late Middle Ages, producing tipple for both clerics and wealthy laypeople. Fittingly the Aberglasney Restoration Team is incorporating some vines into its planting plan. Not an entire, viable vineyard, scribbling the lines of its calligraphy over a whole prime south-facing slope, but the odd vine, grown ornamentally – a memento, a token of homage.

Remember – we are in the Pool Garden, which has its set of controversies as well as its mysteries. The low water level revealed to the restoration team a sort of tump more or less in the middle of the pool, deliberately created at some unknown point in the past as a small island. The experts, trustees and other interested parties split into 'islandists' and 'non-islandists'. Islandists might be influenced by the Victorian school where you built one as a resting place for your ornamental wildfowl (Idris Davies lists egrets, moorhens and snipe remembered from his 1930s childhood), or, more wildly (this is one of William Wilkins's flights of fancy), hoped that archaeology would reveal the base on which some heroic statue – Neptune, perhaps! – was intended to rest and so clinch the argument for an original Renaissance and Italianate inspiration for the Aberglasney gardens. Non-islandists favour the simplicity of an unbroken expanse of water; at most they might consider the retention of a *submerged*, invisible island on which, as Hal Moggridge has suggested, crates of shallow-water varieties of waterlily might be set.

Another topic for debate in the Pool Garden as in other places is the retention of old trees and shrubs. In this garden area there are leggy old box bushes that would once have been clipped into truly boxy shapes, a line of gangly thuja separating us from the Kitchen Garden, a triangle of not-particularly distinguished trees including some ashes. The Radical Restoration School wants a clean sweep: new, carefully chosen specimens. The Gently Does It Approach sees how these trees both echo those on the skyline beyond the garden and confer a paternal air of maturity on raw new planting and unnaturally pristine walls.

Sometimes the plants decide for themselves. One of the most beautiful trees at Aberglasney when the Trust took over was a specimen *Cryptomeria japonica* that made a dramatic feature on the house side of the Pool Garden. An oddity in the context, but one of those compositional flukes that works: it added beauty, dignity. We know not when it was planted, but it can hardly have been before the late nineteenth century. *Cryptomeria japonica* – Japanese red cedar – was introduced to Britain only in 1861, so we perhaps have to allow a decade or so before even the keenest of Welsh gardeners got his seedling. Or was some demon dendrologist keen to impress his neighbours sooner with a novelty? It is certainly rather late for the ambitious John Walters Philipps to have been at work: and he seems to have seen trees in terms of avenues rather than for their individual merit. Among Aberglasney's less well-known ghosts are the tree-planters, whose legacy still enriches the site.

Panorama of the Cloister Garden

It is a well-known fact that exotic conifers tend to grow unpredictably vigorously in high-rainfall areas of the western British Isles. Strange how the exotic, anachronistic cryptomeria was a Good Thing: it was beautiful in itself; it graced its surroundings. Had it survived, its mature dignity would have relieved and compensated the rawness of the restored stonework. In the end the cryptomeria had to be felled as restoration work began: it had become irrevocably diseased in the 1960s and 1970s when David Charles's donkeys were allowed to nibble at the bark, and for all its haunting 'atmosphere' it had to go. The equally exotic thujas dividing the Pond Garden from the Kitchen Garden are rent-a-mob aliens, vegetable breeze-blocks almost as bad in this context as Leyland cypress. They demarcate a necessary barrier, but the further the restoration proceeds and the more presence the stone structures acquire, the grosser their amorphous, outsize, sponge-like greenness comes to seem. More Tree Preservation Orders may need to be challenged.

Let us leave Aberglasney's Pool Garden on a sunny summer's day, in a state that poor Mariana would hardly recognize. The water level is high and the surface is clear, mirror-like, reflecting the sky – ruffled only where newly contoured inlets spout water from a rill to refresh the great still body of the pool, with all the satisfaction that such sights and sounds give the modern observer. Swallows skim the surface of the water as their ancestors have always done in this very spot, whatever the human custodians were

ABOVE A panorama of the Cloister Garden from the parapet at the north-east corner of the garden. The camera pans from a view of the south range (far left) past the long western cloister range (centre) to look past the area where the stairway is being excavated and along the northern parapet.

FOLLOWING PAGES
ABOVE *Looking back
over the Cloister
Garden towards the
house.* BELOW
*Looking over the
Pool Garden towards
Grongar Hill, with
farm buildings
beyond the wall.*

doing to the water level or their surroundings. Observations of the instinctive behaviour of birds like these led John Dyer to make notes for a poem on the theme of 'Nature in ye Wilderness':

Ye Swallow in ye 1st Spring of her year a Novice of Life – builds her nest with wisdom – who tells her her purpose – She lays her Eggs. . .has perfect knowledge to hatch them to feed them and not till they are fledged foresakes them.[25]

We may still marvel at the inbuilt mechanisms that govern the lives, movement and breeding patterns of visiting birds; but we know that when swallows disappear in autumn they migrate to warmer latitudes. In the eighteenth century, when the Dyer family took over Aberglasney, the abrupt disappearance of the swallows was given a different explanation. Dr Johnson's *Dictionary*, among others, reiterated the theory that they plunged underwater to hibernate: 'A number of them conglobulate together, by flying round and round, and then all in a heap throw themselves under water, and lie in the bed of a river. . .'.

Dr Johnson was also pretty scathing about some of John Dyer's poetry.[26] Others were enraptured. It is time now to move on from the Pool Garden in company with this exceptional member of the Dyer dynasty into a different expression, and understanding, of the Natural World.

Panorama from the parapet walk

CHAPTER FOUR

Landscape Bright and Strong

Wilderness and Wood: John Dyer,
Poet of the Picturesque

GARDENS OF A DIFFERENT CHARACTER occupy the roughly sock-shaped piece of Aberglasney territory farthest from the mansion, with its toe pointing westwards. Here, just about out of sight of solid reminders in the form of manmade stone walls, we can collude with the gardeners' and the poets' professional deception and pretend for a while that we are in the realms of nature. Here within the soft canopy of deciduous trees, their trunks barring out the view of bright green farmland beyond, we can pretend, too, that we are deep in an immense wood, and that Aberglasney's acres extend once more to the hidden horizons.

> And here a silent, quiet walk is made,
> Straight onward running in the green wood shade;
> How beautiful upon soft mossy beds,
> These living pillars rise with noble heads.[1]

To leave the Pool Garden at its lower side is to leave the introspection of the walled and well-tended enclosures and step outside into what is more obviously part of the landscape, as the ground slopes away into a deepening wooded dingle before rising again in the sweep that becomes Grongar Hill. The sometimes graceful, sometimes abrupt topography of the Towy valley has always charmed and fascinated spectators. The pioneering landscapists were impressed: Lancelot 'Capability' Brown's comment on Dynevor Park – then known as Newton House – when he was invited to advise on improvements in 1775 was that 'Nature has been truly bountiful, and Art has done no harm'. A couple of miles downriver geology has moulded another salient hill formation with the kind of panoramic outlook that invited the building of early hillforts. Some spectators were rather downbeat about its character. 'Grongar Hill has derived from nature nothing to distinguish it from other hills,' was one verdict, – 'its fame is entirely the gift of the poet'.[2]

We shall see how (and perhaps why) John Dyer of Aberglasney (painter, poet, parson and, incidentally, coiner of the phrase 'from the cradle to the grave') put this eminence of only moderately arresting profile firmly on the cultural map. The sight of Grongar was probably imprinted on his mind from his earliest infancy.

The Dyers, whom we met *en famille* in the previous chapter, brought Aberglasney

In the Stream Garden. . .the naturally damp ground is indulged and the art and artifice of gardening conjure a luxurious 'natural' spread of water- and moisture-loving plants. . .

into the eighteenth century. Sometime between 1710 and 1720, as we have seen, Robert Dyer senior gave Aberglasney mansion its new north façade. His son John Dyer gave it something less concrete, more intangible, but in a way far more enduring. Fame. His acclaimed poem 'Grongar Hill' put this corner of the Towy valley – indeed, this corner of Wales – firmly on the cultural map. Grongar became flagged as a real place made familiar through art. No coach-tours and tea-towels in Dyer's day, but an early waft of the same scent of success. Soon no Traveller penning a Tour (and there were many of them in the late 1700s, and even more to come) could pass from Carmarthen to Llandeilo without a salute (or an apostrophe!) to Grongar and the poet Dyer, although few named, and even fewer visited, his early home, Aberglasney. He gained admirers from the Wesleys to Wordsworth, from James Thomson to Dylan Thomas (whose Reverend Eli Jenkins, bard of Milk Wood, gives Grongar a mention), and many more besides. He was also translated, so that poet and place gained a parallel following among Welsh-speaking fellow-countrymen.

Aberglasney became famous simply for being the home of the poet; John Dyer specifically named it in 'The Country Walk', a cousin-poem to 'Grongar Hill'.[3] From the first publication of these two key poems, Aberglasney gained reflected glory by being the place from which one might, as did the poet, both admire Grongar Hill from a distance and set out to explore its slopes and prospects. (A third option suggested, only half in devilment, is that when Dyer refers to woods 'where Echo talks', he speaks from his own boyhood experience. We will explore this possibility when we reach the heady heights of Chapter Six.)

The actuality of John Dyer's relationship with the landscape surrounding Grongar and Aberglasney shines through the conventions and archaisms that tend to dim for today's readers some of the clarity and freshness of his vision. William Gilpin, that philosopher of picturesque theory, might exclaim that Dyer had got his colours and perspective wrong, in parts, but he acknowledged that 'Dyer is for the first time in poetry giving us a real hill'.[4] There is a down-to-earth physicality about John Dyer's presence in these poems. When, in 'The Country Walk', Dyer writes 'Up Grongar Hill I labour now. . .' we find ourselves panting alongside him up the steep slopes, and relieved to pause and 'breathe a little' when we get to the top. From here we gain that most useful prospect of the establishment newly refurbished by Robert Dyer, attorney, late of Carmarthen:

See, below, the pleasant dome,
The poet's pride, the poet's home,
Which the sunbeams shine upon,
To the even, from the dawn.
See her woods, where Echo talks,
Her gardens trim, her terrace walks,
Her wildernesses, fragrant brakes,
Her gloomy bowers and shining lakes,
Keep, ye gods, this humble seat,
For ever pleasant, private, neat.

Let us leave John Dyer to his poetic contemplation and return for the moment to the present. We find ourselves in one of Aberglasney's lower-lying and 'more natural' areas. In the cluster of upper gardens, geometry holds sway: the natural contours of the ground are ruled over by rectangular configurations of walls, paths, buildings and beds, while underneath springs and streams are controlled and directed – buried in land-drains or channelled to feed the pool. Here they emerge and show us clearly where watercourses have carved (and are still carving) deep clefts into the soft, malleable land, reminding us in microcosm how the whole valley – the entire landscape – is shaped by the scouring effects of water. Where the land folds steeply down little sunlight reaches the ground, and the shade is deepened by tree cover. The plants that choose to live here are selective and specialized: no place here for rank vegetable *hoi polloi*. We tread on sparse denizens of the woodland floor. Ostensibly we are now leaving the ordered province governed by the gardener and entering a wider world where nature – earth, wind, water and sunlight – holds sway.

The Restoration Trust has christened these adjacent areas the Stream Garden and Pigeon House Wood. Outside the civilized walled gardens Aberglasney's many acres of estate land are reduced to this little patch of countryside. It is barely a token, a postage-stamp sized patch of woodland and a burbling streamlet. But its trees grow like John Dyer's living pillars and by half-closing your eyes you can blot out the presence of the boundary fencing. In this state of stillness (low-flying military aircraft and local farm machinery permitting) you might even hear the descendants of John Dyer's thrush, listen for the poet's blessed Quiet, and indulge a sense of spurious continuity with the wood where Lewis Glyn Cothi's 'young oaks' once grew. (Spurious because this wood is probably not at all ancient.)

You might picture Aberglasney figures of old passing through trees like these – generations of squires and keepers with guns under their arm; ladies of the house bearing sketchbooks; odd-jobbing Catherine John earning her daily sixpence by gathering acorns in a chill November; other servants, perhaps, guiding cartloads of ice from the frozen pond up to the ice-house that some believe was on the side of Grongar

Hill; Robert Archer Dyer contemplating his plan 'to plant ye sides [of Grongar] with firr [sic]'; hopeful Thomas Phillips and aspiring John Walters Philipps early in the following century checking the progress of their newly planted saplings. . .

Then there is detective work to be done. Take Pigeon House Wood. Most trees in this small wood are growing up tall and straight-trunked, as they would do in the close competition of neighbours, periodically thinned and tended. But several older oaks have spreading crowns, indicating that they acquired their free shapes in open ground, before the area was densely wooded as it is now. Some are on hedge banks and might have been boundary markers. Low banks run here and there through the area, defining lost fields or enclosures but no longer acting as effective barriers. How old are they? How long has this been a wood? And why the name Pigeon House Wood? We must explore this later.

The wood was very likely not here when Aberglasney's most celebrated son, John Dyer, made his way between the mansion and Grongar Hill, although he may well have passed some of those oaks. We shall follow our hero as he heads for London, Rome and the professionalism which allowed him to achieve success and acclaim – although he was drawn there by the ambition to be a painter rather than a wordsmith. The circles in which he moved and the people he met present a fascinating cast of characters, but we who are interested in Aberglasney will ever be on the lookout for hints and clues that might provide us with more missing pieces for our jigsaw puzzle.

John Dyer did not spend his childhood at Aberglasney, but he must have known the place. If before the family acquired Aberglasney he lived or stayed in his forebears' house of Abersannan, he will have had a splendid sideways-on view of Grongar Hill which lies almost due south. By the time Robert Dyer's building works on the new Aberglasney mansion were under way, John Dyer was probably already attending Westminster School and his older brother Robert had gone up to Balliol. However, the autobiographical fragment quoted previously hints at the likelihood that Aberglasney was already a presence in the family mythology, and not just any newly acquired property. It did become John Dyer's home after he left Westminster (perhaps as early as 1714, or possibly two or three years later) and until 1720 or 21, when his brother took over the Dyer estates after their father's death. During those years back in Carmarthenshire John studied law, presumably in the family firm.

Tradition has it that John Dyer's father opposed his artistic ambitions, but he cannot have thwarted them; in turn the father's hard-nosed business conduct may well have deepened John Dyer's instinctive aversion to the law.

The poet was a mild and gentle person, and throughout his life held humanitarian ideals. What he observed in his father's practices, and they were probably general among legal men of that day, would obviously have offended him. Painting. . .was his first love, while he was studying with his father, and would ultimately have led him away from the law, but the definite dislike of the law with which tradition has endowed the poet may be traced back. . .to the character of the first Robert Dyer of Aberglasney, Gent.[5]

We find John was already in London in 1719, before his father died. He had already experimented with poetry while he lived at Aberglasney. His first version of 'Grongar Hill' was composed, according to the poet, in a wood; local people used to point out the very blackthorn bush under which it was conceived[6] and so is rooted in the landscape of his home, although it went through various modifications later, in London and in Rome. The topic of the intricate verse of the 1716 version is a comparison of natural and artificial architecture. Dyer's thoughtful muse claims to find more inspiration among the 'living pillars' of the trees in the 'green wood shade' than among extravagant edifices like St Peter's in Rome or Babel's towering pile. While he admires the polished marble and the sculptor's art, it is 'Nature's rustic work' that excites his wonder and in the end prevails. John Dyer's trees, with their 'intermingling leaves that softly twine,/ And roundly branching, from their pillars join/ To form a living roof, and shade the tuneful Nine' seem to have an affinity with Lewis Glyn Cothi's 'young oaks reaching up to the sky'. Dyer's 'tuneful Nine' muses make a pleasing echo with Glyn Cothi's 'nine green gardens', too. But John Dyer was not destined to stay in this pastoral, sylvan setting: the outside world beckoned.

Pursuit of an artistic vocation took John Dyer to London as a pupil of the eminent Jonathan Richardson, one of the most successful painters of his day, but now better remembered as a writer on art and a collector of drawings: he is said to have coined the term 'connoisseur' in the modern sense. 'Richardson. . .believed that a painter should be a full man, well read, observant of nature, conversant with the best human company, because the quality of a man shows in his work'.[7] Not least, Richardson imbued Dyer with his delight in Milton's poetry; Dyer responded by filling sixty pages of his Commonplace book with quotations from *Paradise Lost* 'showing a predilection for descriptions of trees and waterfalls' and absorbing Milton's metric forms into his verse. William Wordsworth, an admirer of Dyer, later linked the two poets: 'In point of imagination, and purity of style, I am not sure he is not superior to any writer of verse since the time of Milton.'[8]

There were more worldly delights. Richardson's pupils and their friends were a lively crew and soon Dyer was meeting like-minded people at Serle's Coffee House in Carey Street – 'the place to rendezvous to all that live near it' in the words of the essayist Sir Richard Steele – and helping to form a club that hoped to render itself 'considerable in the commonwealth of wit and letters'. How splendid to find the future poet of the picturesque on the threshold of his career in the close company of Steele, who with Joseph Addison and through *The Tatler*, *The Spectator* and the Kit-Kat Club, had provided the literary lubrication to oil the wheels that were beginning to revolve into the English Landscape Style. The friendship between Dyer and Steele was more than the acquaintance of coffee-house commensals. Richardson was a link – he had done Steele's portrait in *Spectator* days,[9] but Dyer might well already have known Steele from back home. Steele married Mary Scurlock, only child and heiress of a family of rich Carmarthen tradesmen who would certainly have been known to the seventeenth-century Dyers who practised law in the town.[10] Sir Richard Steele in turn gives us a brief portrait of John Dyer, where he 'found in the neighbourhood two young men of his own kidney, two young poets, John and Robert Dyer, to shoulder the hours with'. John Dyer, from Aberglasney, was described as 'the more picturesque of the two, with lofty forehead and long hair waving back from it'.[11]

However, we must not linger in Wales following up the latter stages of the Steele–Dyer friendship. We must hurry back to London and next join the young John Dyer as he enters into more heady company. Dyer now became a key figure in the leading London literary circle of the 1720s, which included the winsome Mrs Martha Fowke Sansom (known by the pseudonym Clio, presumably to advertise her role as muse) and James Thomson (whose *The Seasons* later became an inspiration to the Picturesque movement). Again poetry was the result. The endless exchanges of mutually flattering verse engendered fluency (as well as other gratification) in the writers and provide the biographer with smatterings of promising detail and comment that help in the triangulation process of mapping their various lives and movements. This early Georgian fast set 'seem to have seen themselves as living a life of courtly Platonic romance rather alien to their time,' writes Belinda Humfrey: and they drank tea rather than coffee while composing love-poems to Clio. Clio's charms may occasionally have been tested in the flesh. Samuel Johnson saw her in a more cynical light as 'a lady once too well known'. Dyer played the gallant and paid earnest court in verse, but almost certainly kept his distance.

In mid-1724 Dyer broke away from this steamy atmosphere to spend a year in Italy studying painting. He visited Tivoli, Florence, Naples and Venice, but Rome made the deepest impression. The fascination of observing and drawing its ruins compensated for the loneliness Dyer felt. His painterly perceptions crystallized into the powerful poem 'The Ruins of Rome'.

To those of us who seek to make the acquaintance of John Dyer primarily because of our interest in

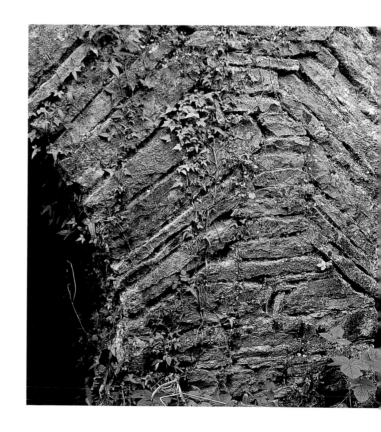

BELOW *Over the years the stone structures at Aberglasney became coloured with creeping colonies of lichens. Visiting Rome, John Dyer saw in such mellowness 'a certain charm that follows the sweep of time'. Repair work has effaced much of Aberglasney's lichen cover, but the remnants will creep back and recreate that 'certain disjointedness and moulder in the stones' that pleased his painterly eye.*

ABOVE *John Dyer (1699–1757, probably a self-portrait) whose father bought Aberglasney when he was a child. He rejected the law for a career as a painter but achieved lasting fame as a poet. He vividly described the local landscape in 'Grongar Hill' and in 'The Country Walk' sang the praises of 'the poet's pride, the poet's home' – Aberglasney – putting both poet and place on the cultural map.*

Aberglasney, his home of a few years as he approached adulthood, his stay in Rome seems peculiarly significant. On the one hand we picture the Carmarthenshire lad not simply living among the ruins and the relics of a past civilization but actively, creatively absorbing their aura and resolving his reaction into an eloquent, complex philosophical statement. At Aberglasney, on a somewhat different scale, we find ourselves seeking to make a similar resolution. Aberglasney, like Rome, is absolutely the product of the past – in this case an enigmatic, ill-documented history that leaves many questions unanswered. Like Rome it has built structures and ruins. The scale is different – the comparison perhaps absurd – but the impact of each on the unwary has similarities and conjures echoes. In some sense we stand in relation to Aberglasney's gatehouse tower and mysterious cloisters as John Dyer did to the arches along the Sacred Way: they inspire awe and wonder in the observer. Those of us who saw Aberglasney in romantic (but dangerous) decline before its repair was undertaken also share Dyer's sharp pleasure at the mellowing effects of time, with Welsh ferns substituting for Mediterranean myrtle:

> There is a certain charm that follows the sweep of time, and I can't help thinking the triumphal arches more beautiful now than ever they were, there is a certain greenness, with many other colours, and a certain disjointedness and moulder among the stones, something so pleasing in their weeds and tufts of myrtle, and something in them altogether so greatly wild, that mingling with art, and blotting out the traces of disagreeable squares and angles, adds certain beauties that could not be before imagined, which is the cause of surprise that no modern building can give.[12]

Dyer worked on the final version of 'Grongar Hill' as well as 'The Ruins' when in Italy, conjuring the Towy landscape in contrast to that of the Tiber, but found no domestic echoes of arches or cloisters to prompt comparisons or reverberations with the courtyard back home. The blending of art and nature he saw in Rome evoked no memories of home. For Dyer the structures at Aberglasney must have been mundane.

Modern and mundane, because they had been built a century or more ago and therefore had not acquired the patina of true antiquity – in fact they were simply rather old hat. Or unmentioned because they did not yet exist? One of the theories ventured by experts in the early restoration days held that the Dyers were the garden-makers, between 1710 and 1742, and that the origin of the courtyard was 'linked to the Italian experiences of the poet, John Dyer, and the early stages of the fashion for ruins in the landscape'.[13] Visitors often say that at first sight they took the structures at Aberglasney to be some kind of eighteenth-century pastiche. These reactions seems to presuppose John Dyer rushing home to Carmarthenshire waving his sketchbooks and enthusing his landlord brother Robert about classical architecture and brooding ruins. 'Do build a cryptoporticus, Bob! Here's what they look like, and have it made a bit tumble-down – ruins are just the latest thing!' On his return from Italy in 1725 John Dyer did spend the summer at Llangathen, and he continued to divide his time between Wales and London for some years. However, it is unlikely that he exercised the sort of influence on Robert that would lead to extensive feats of garden building. All three younger brothers fell out with the new heir of Aberglasney over the non-payment of their inheritance from their father, and there was an acerbic, but successful, lawsuit in 1727–8, in which John's early training in the law seems to have trumped that of his barrister brother. John was probably *persona non grata* at Aberglasney after that.

One visit by John Dyer to his home territory must be recorded. In July 1727 Dyer witnessed Sir Richard Steele's will. By the time the two friends met again in Carmarthen, Steele (as a subscriber to Richard Savage's *Miscellanies*) had read and enjoyed John Dyer's 'Country Walk' and 'Grongar Hill', and 'their friendship deepened from there. "Your peopling pencil a new world can give," wrote one of Dyer's admirers. The young poet was a lover of scenery in verse when no other writer regarded it, and Sir Richard was ever an applauder of an independent spirit.'[14]

By now the crippled Steele had taken up residence in another of the Scurlocks' properties in Carmarthen, which later became the Ivy Bush Inn – 'a gentleman's seat on the banks of the river, [and] one of the best in the town. The rooms command a charming reach of the river. . .'.[15] It is pleasing to think of the Sir Richard contemplating the Towy and finding satisfaction in the handsome pictures of nature as he had done years ago when writing through the eye of *The Spectator*. Two years after John Dyer witnessed his will, the chairborne Sir Richard is found going to watch the dancing on the Castle Green (and ordering a new gown for the girl who he thought danced the best).[16] He died in September 1729 and was buried in the Scurlock vault in St Peter's Church, Carmarthen. Like John Dyer, Steele seems to have divided his time between Wales and London, but unlike Dyer, Wales is where he ended up.

Carmarthenshire never became John Dyer's home again. For some years he divided his time between London and an itinerant life as a painter in Wales and the border counties. By 1730 he had moved to the farm called Mapleton (in Herefordshire) owned by his maiden aunt, Elizabeth Cocks and part of his grandfather's estate which he was to inherit. Farming now took up much of his attention, though poetry remained a

Stream Garden and Pigeon House Wood

ABOVE *Stream Garden and Pigeon House Wood are vestiges of many acres of land once owned by the Aberglasney estate. Surrounded by farmland, they link the garden and the so-called 'natural landscape' of the countryside.*

RIGHT *The Glasnai stream burbles away towards the Towy through neglected woodland at the property's lowest contours. The continuity of this semi-natural habitat means that native plant species may find refuge here.*

steady strand in his life: he wrote, and periodically published, almost to the end of his life. He also maintained a lively intellectual curiosity, copying telling excerpts from contemporary (and classical) writers into his notebooks for their own interest as well as for their possible contribution to various projects he had in mind. They are interspersed with notes recording the religious feeling which gradually crystallized into a vocation. He became ordained and spent the latter part of his life as a farming parson in the alien landscapes of Leicestershire and of the fens of East Anglia.

It is tempting to follow this interesting man through the remaining twenty-odd years of his life after he leaves our Aberglasney stage. In 1738 he married Sarah Ensor, reputedly descended from Shakespeare's brother. He had a son and three daughters who are said to have died without issue but in fact there were, and are, descendants through the female line. Declining health did little to dim his perennial intellectual curiosity. We would find him combining his clerical duties with ambitious plans to compile a 'Commercial Map' of Britain, a project which involved extensive reading. Many of the far-seeing ideas he proposed were later implemented, such as linking key waterways by building canals to facilitate the transport of coal. He also kept Wales in mind, deploring the poor condition of its ports and communications: 'Aberystwyth in its present Condition, is hardly to be named.' He suggested improving it as a port and building a good road from there to the clothing town of Leominster, to stimulate a trade between westbound hops and cider and eastbound Irish wool. The route was later followed by the A44.

Then there is his four-part poem *The Fleece*, for which Wordsworth called him 'aimiable Dyer' and wrote the following salute 'To the Poet, John Dyer':

> *Bard of the Fleece! whose skilful genius made*
> *That work a living landscape fair and bright;*
> *Nor hallow'd less with musical delight*
> *Than those soft scenes, thro' which thy childhood strayed. . .*

Its fourth and final book was published in 1757, the year of his death amid 'the air of a fenny country, where I have been, for the most part. . .without health, without books, and without proper conversation'. An exaggeration, perhaps: he had the constant encouragement of some of his oldest friends, who had supported his work on *The Fleece*, and his library was extensive. Dyer's biographer Belinda Humfrey calls *The Fleece* 'a tapestry or living landscape of his own life'. From our standpoint of investigating Aberglasney and its garden oddities, it is tempting to comb the *The Fleece* for information that might help us understand the influence of Dyer's Carmarthenshire origins on his thinking. We must resist these distractions and *revenons à nos moutons*. Is there any evidence that in the half-dozen places he lived after leaving Aberglasney John Dyer used Aberglasney as a touchstone in his garden-making?

Just a little is known of the contemporary gardening influences that John Dyer encountered. He made a visit to Blenheim Palace early on, when the formality of the garden design by Vanbrugh, Bridgeman and Henry Wise held sway. It took place sometime before 1722, when the first Duke of Marlborough died: he saw the famous tapestries there, and wrote about the sad dotage of the duke, but did not mention gardens.[17] He read Batty Langley's *New Principles of Gardening*, published in 1728 but influential for another twenty years and more. At some point Dyer visited Stowe – perhaps in 1733. Throughout Dyer's adulthood it was being transformed by Viscount Cobham into one of the world's most famous landscape gardens and here he would have encountered the successive input of Vanbrugh, Bridgeman, Kent and James Gibbs; after 1741 he might have made the acquaintance of the head gardener, Lancelot 'Capability' Brown. But we do not know whether Dyer acted upon any of these formative encounters.

The storyteller lights with keen hope on a brief entry in John Dyer's notebooks entitled 'On Gardens'. Will it reveal how early exposure to Aberglasney's built structures – already outmoded by the time he was writing in the 1730s – formed his future aesthetic? Will it confirm him, with his love of the natural landscape of his homeland, as a 'natural' in the gardening landscape tradition in its very earliest dawnings? The result is disappointing. No dazzling revelations, no key piece of jigsaw enigma that might decode a whole missing corner of the picture. Rather, two apparently contradictory arguments, and delivered in the liverish, jaundiced tones of one irritated perhaps by the heartburn for which he jotted down remedies in the same notebook. On the one hand he appears to deplore the artifice of over-structured gardens (cloistered galleries? yew tunnels?) that 'tailors and carpenters' might be expected to make, preferring the free 'asymmetry' of the Chinese; on the other he seems to advocate the dullest layout comprising 'borders round about [a] field'.

Of Gardens

We are but little we are mean we are blind we have no nobleness of Imagination no Eye for Simplicity Nature & Beauty in anything (I speak as to the general taste) except in matters of direct necessity things that serve to feed or clothe the Body.

To learn Architecture Painting Music – we must go out of our foggy Island into some foreign country & for Poetry & some of the nobler parts of learning we must Search ye books of ye antients.

Yet after all we will not see what is as plain as the Sun – We write as if we never read Greek or Latin and build as if none of us ever travelled to Rome or Athens.

In chusing our Situations & laying out our Gardens one wd think we consulted our Taylors & Carpenters though our very Tars who return from China give us descriptions of Gardens in that beautiful Country wch far exceed any of those artificial Scenes in Europe.[18]

He ends by alluding to the Bible – and to the image of the field of Ephron in Genesis, chapter 24, with 'the Cave that was in the end of the Field and the Trees that were in all the borders round about the Field'. Simplicity itself: dullness, even: borders surrounding an open field. Perhaps it was the serpentine fussiness of modern designers that he inveighed against. He was certainly inveighing about something. The fragment ends with stunning vehemence: 'The truth is this we see like Pismires.'[19]

Whatever his concepts of design and layout, his husbandry was evidently of a thoroughly practical kind. He began to compile alphabetical notes on tasks to be done in the garden and about the farm. Livestock and crops were equally in his mind – sheep and hops are among subjects dealt with at some length. An entry entitled 'Trees' includes detailed notes about ways of propagating various evergreens – pyracantha, holly, yew, laurustinus – but offers no hint of how and where they were to be planted.

It is time to call off what is becoming a wild-goose chase. John Dyer has strayed too far away from our theme, and it is time to admit that we are unlikely to discover in his available work some master-key that will open up hitherto unknown evidence about how Aberglasney influenced him, or what he thought when he recalled Aberglasney in his later years. Instead of seeking detailed forensic evidence, we should perhaps stand back and allow the spirit of his poetry to imbue our quest. His was the day when 'Nature' was becoming the important influence in gardening and landscape, ousting the artifice of the gardens of the Stuarts. After a quarter of a millennium the 'natural' in gardening is still a byword. We can find it again in Aberglasney today.

So our time machine brings us back to the present, and deposits us in what is called the Stream Garden. This first area – a shallow, elongated half-moon of open ground adjoining the Pool Garden – offers an intermediate stage between the regular structures of the overtly manmade garden and the woodland, where lines are only as straight as nature chooses – a slender trunk drawn towards the light, the angled sunbeams filtering between branches towards the earth. The past of this piece of ground is a mystery. In Aberglasney's early days it might have been an orchard or a nuttery, or perhaps the laundry-drying ground, where the washing was spread out on clipped bushes, preferably aromatic-leaved evergreens but here quite likely gorse, to bleach in the sun. In John Dyer's day – when first his father, then his brother, and then his nephew Robert Archer Dyer owned the property – this would have been the perfect place for an example of one of those strangely tame tracts of garden that used to be honoured with the alarming-sounding name of 'wilderness'. Wandering the winding paths between banks of shrubs (often aromatic) and trees (often for fruit) that screened the general layout from view, the Dyers' eighteenth-century contemporaries would seek the intended *frisson* of momentarily feeling oneself lost in this minor labyrinth or might indulge in Rousseauesque reveries on nature and innocence.

Or perhaps in previous incarnations what is now the Stream Garden did play more functional roles. Although damp, this ground would have been too fertile and precious to be 'wasted' in the days when the gardens of a substantial estate were hard-pressed to grow enough food to sustain an extended household. Watercress flourished quite recently in the running water. In better-drained ground to each side of the stream fruit and vegetables might be cultivated. Perhaps the northern end of this piece of ground was primarily functional, the southern end more ornamental. Somewhere, when Thomas Phillips bought the property, he will have found the frames that were glazed in readiness for his arrival – perhaps here; somewhere, two generations later, were to be found the 'large Pinery, Melon Grounds and. . .Glass Houses' mentioned in the advertisement of 1872. Glazed frames or glasshouses appear on maps from mid-century on, towards the northern, farmyard end of the area, and quite a tall glazed structure – more a glasshouse than a frame – is visible above the wall to the right of the weeping ash in a view of the Pool Garden taken by photographer C.S. Allen in about 1870. Another two generations on, a drawing by Idris Davies shows cold frames and a potting shed around here on the eve of World War Two.

Today where a greenhouse once stood, you now stand to admire new planting. A contemporary version of naturalism prevails. This intermediate area has become the Stream Garden: the naturally damp ground is indulged and the art and artifice of gardening conjure a luxurious 'natural' spread of water- and moisture-loving planting. Conditions like these allow gardeners to achieve 'melting-pot' multinational harmonies in the plant world. Because they naturalize so well and look so much at home, lush, large-leaved plants from wet places all over the world combine happily in British gardens. The League of Nations in the Stream Garden includes a fair contingent of Orientals: the giant cowslip, *Primula florindae*, comes from China and Tibet. Two rodgersias – Chinese *Rodgersia aesculifolia* and Japanese *R. podophylla* – have contrasting leaf forms; their relative *Astilboides tabularis* from China is underplanted with a form of bloodroot, *Sanguinaria canadensis* from north-east America. *Iris sibirica* is from central Europe as well as Russia. *Gunnera manicata* comes from Brazil. Mimulus is another New World genus. Idris Davies records the ornamental rhubarb, *Rheum palmatum*, growing here in the old days; it is from China.

This kind of planting perfectly celebrates the philosophy that William Robinson expressed in his bestselling *The Wild Garden* (published in 1870 – about the time C.S. Allen was photographing at Aberglasney) – that of encouraging 'the placing of perfectly hardy exotic plants under conditions where they will thrive without further care' – and that has become the credo of the 'natural' gardener ever since. It is quite a paradox that the enlightened William Robinson is also at the root of one of contemporary gardening's (and one of Aberglasney's) most persistent problems. Its name is Japanese knotweed. Before you undertake any exciting new creative planting you have to eradicate every last bit. This pernicious plant had colonized this moist streamside area as well as other parts of the Aberglasney gardens.

LEFT *A strip of no-man's-land slopes down between the formal Pool Garden and the wood. Once fruit trees and glasshouses stood here and watercress was grown. Now the naturally damp ground is being prepared for a display of moisture-loving ornamental plants and to become the new Stream Garden.*

RIGHT *The mansion is clad in scaffolding; work on the high crenellated wall beyond the pool is well underway. The low wall separating the Pool Garden from the Stream Garden has yet to be stripped of its mantle of ivy and made safe, and the pool's overflow waits to be moulded into a naturalistic water feature.*

First introduced to Britain in the 1820s as a fodder plant and as a garden ornamental, it has spread beyond belief, despite being sterile in these islands, fragments of underground rhizomes grow into new plants, which then silently creep and colonize and consolidate their domain. Its Welsh name is *pysen saethwr* – peashooter![20] William Robinson knew it as *Polygonum cuspidatum* (nowadays it's *Fallopia japonica*). Along with its cousin the giant knotweed he admittedly rated it 'among the plants that cannot be put in the garden without fear of their overrunning other things', but it was understatement indeed when he summed the pair up: 'They are fine plants for deep soils and can certainly take care of themselves.' Repeated applications of glyphosate have put paid (we hope) to Aberglasney's knotweed problem. But doesn't William Robinson twitch in his grave at the curses of the gardeners who have to deal with the over-vigorous heritage?

Now the ground tilts sharply down and to the south, carved by Nant Glasnai, of whose presence as a rivulet in its own right we now become aware – it has accumulated its due tributes of channels and drains and now comes out into the open as a stream. One of the delights of a large proportion of Welsh place-names is what they tell you about the lie of the land: the Eskimos are supposed to have coined a plethora of names for many different kinds of snow, but Welsh really does have scores of names for the specific topography of hill and dale. A name inspired by some sort of eminence will often tell you whether the hilltop is wooded or bald, the steepness and shape and character of its slopes, the nature of the valley cut into its flanks, and so on. Another kind of name derives from watercourses. Thus, ever since arriving at Aberglasney, we have been looking out for a river named something like Glasney and for its *aber* or estuary (or, since we are inland, confluence). Even the tiniest streams have names. Many stream and river names end in the suffix '*ai*' (or '*ei*') and its variant '*nai*', and the '*glas*' element is likely to refer to the colour of the water or the river bed.[21] Now here the precision of Welsh topographical nomenclature gives way to an amazing vagueness, for the portmanteau adjective *glas* can mean blue, or green, or grey, or simply pale. Presumably water can be all of those things. Often at Aberglasney it's a muddy brown.

This lowest-lying part of contemporary Aberglasney is one of those wooded dingles that are often vestiges of ancient woodland, being too steep or too marshy to bring into cultivation. This is not to say that the trees you see growing today are either native or old (the hand of man prevails here too). Estate woodlands were managed by coppicing, felling and replanting over generations, both for timber and as cover for game. However, the continuity of the presence of trees often makes these areas act as refugia for native flora – lichens and mosses and the higher plants and mushrooms. The ground flora we find in the woodland – dog's mercury, ramsons etc. – indicates a base-rich soil where we might look out for interesting plants such as green hellebore, herb paris, lily-of-the-valley, that are known to grow wild in woods not far from here.

We look up from examining detail and consider the wider landscape. This northern side – the 'right bank' – of the Towy is indeed the edge of a belt of carboniferous limestone. It slices south-west to north-east across southern Carmarthenshire like the slash in a vulgar fraction, separating a desert of poorer, acidic Silurian shales to the north and west from the richer, more complex rocks of South Wales. Its south-eastern face borders the coalfields. The Towy's course down to Carmarthen has cut into the harder rock, leaving occasional outliers. It's an ancient and long-acclaimed landscape. The broad, fertile, welcoming watermeadows of the Towy have enticed incomers and invaders since the earliest times (its aspect and accessibility contrasting favourably with endless miles of unfathomable hill-country round about). In days of conflict greedy Romans and Normans and English used the river valley as easy access, so defensive castles sprouted at salient points. In calmer, more prosperous times rocky fastnesses were relegated to history and the picturesque, and a new series of more amenable sites were chosen as the seats of the gentry. The process was one of constant upgrading of the more desirable properties. The new popularity boom in the late eighteenth century, found landowners inspired anew by the vision of the picturesque 'capabilities' of the landscape. The wealth of contemporaneous nabobs gave new status to both Middleton and Aberglasney. We might mark the parallel local boom in the late twentieth century, as both Middleton and Aberglasney are blessed with unexpected new incarnations. Now, however, new criteria make this environment appreciated for its clean air, moist oceanic climate – and lack of population pressure.

In the midst of this dramatic landscape context of the Towy valley and its historic houses, Aberglasney essentially remains somewhat inward-looking. Even its landscape views are limited ones, glimpsed over and through those high enclosing walls. Before we make our way back towards those walls, where we have a date with the people who succeeded the Dyers as owners, we must just tie up one or two loose ends that take us a little way outside Aberglasney's present-day boundaries, and a little way into the past.

Earlier in the chapter we promised to investigate the name Pigeon House Wood. A dwelling called Pigeon House Cottage lies along the lane between Aberglasney and Grongar with its own garden and yard. It was once an intrinsic part of the estate. A nearby field of nearly four acres is called Pigeon Close on the Tithe Map. If the estate ever had a real pigeon house – a noisy, smelly working dovecote providing the traditional crops of squabs for the table and dung for the gardens – it would be located somewhere here, the functional end of the Aberglasney complex where the working farmyard with the pigsties and hay barn used to be. There was a flurry of 'improvement' to something called the Pigeon House in the early 1800s. It sounds as if a functional building was being spruced up for a new, ornamental role. Such a transformation was the height of fashion, since the practice of breeding pigeons for the table was in steep decline by that time and dovecotes built or refurbished around then developed a distinctly ornamental aspect. John Philipps's efforts to prepare Aberglasney for the arrival of his brother from India seem to have taken every detail into account. Lead costing £2 11s. 9d. was purchased for repairing the roof, which now incorporated a cupola (the work cost £2 19s. 9d.) and was surmounted by a vane and eagle (cost two guineas).[22] This was clearly to be something of an eyecatcher: we should look for its location somewhere clearly visible from the windows of the mansion or from the parapet walk, but nothing of any ornamental dovecote seems to have survived the nineteenth century.

A ruin near Pigeon House Cottage has mystified some investigators: a conduit house or, confusingly, a chapel? The chapel designation doesn't hold water: the building, known as 'Bishop Rudd's Bath', does: 'its original construction specially adapting it for bathing use – a dressing room, with fireplace, opening on to a bricked tank that occupies the rest of the interior.'[23] Antiquarianism flourished briefly in the early 1900s when Colonel Mayhew had taken Aberglasney in hand and keen visitors were taken to the bath house 'through the kindly guidance of our enthusiastic hostess', Mrs Mayhew. The waters were 'said to partake of a medicinal character,' and the visit's recorder speculated as to whether the use of the spring might be of considerably greater antiquity than the time of Bishop Rudd.[24]

In the 1920s a pen-portrait of Aberglasney by a distant member of the Rudd family included a detailed sketch of the bathhouse, and somewhat affectionately pictured it in use by the Bishop:

> About half a mile away, lies the now ruined little building which is known as Bishop Rudd's Bath. It stands now in the garden of a cottage, but in those days was probably included in the private grounds of Aberglasney. Within the building is still to be seen a ruined but spacious tank in the floor, with steps down into it, and still supplied through the original spout by the spring of water which flows from above the building. A small fireplace occupies one corner and a few of the original flooring tiles are still *in situ*. It was here that tradition asserted the Bishop came morning by morning during his residence at Aberglasney for his daily ablutions. Possibly the early morning plunge into the waters of the Swale in his youth may have created a habit of his lifetime to which the walk to the 'Bath' and its icy spring of water may have formed the nearest possible approach. The practice betokens a hardy northern constitution.[25]

At the opposite end of Aberglasney we have 'Bishop Rudd's Walk' – the short-cut he took from the house to Llangathen parish church. Now along with the all the other inhabitants we have imagined passing in this direction among the trees perhaps we can picture the Bishop heading down this way (towel in hand?) on his morning constitutional, towards his bath house nestling in the lower slopes of Grongar Hill.

CHAPTER FIVE

The Pleasures of Good Order

The Walled Gardens
and the Philipps Era

T HE LARGE WALLED KITCHEN GARDEN is profusely stocked with choice fruit trees,' declaimed the *Tenby Observer* of 14 November 1872, offering Aberglasney as a most desirable house to let. Between the lines of fruit trees in the large walled garden we can also picture the neat rows of vegetables and salads, the tended strawberry beds (runners marshalled into place), colourful clumps of cutting flowers and the punctuating hardware of bell cloches and forcing jars, all within the strict cruciform pattern of box-edged paths. A kitchen garden in its Victorian heyday (with the pinery, vinery and melon ground that the advertisement also boasted) was the power-house supplying the family, the household and its visitors with almost everything it needed, and the head gardener with justifiable pride. Mid-century Aberglasney's productive gardens would have been in fine fettle under the ambitious John Walters Philipps and his lively entourage, which included three marriageable daughters. By the time the advertisement was published in 1872 things had become rather quieter. Most family events were taking place off-stage. The late patriarch's only grandchild was about to marry that December. Somehow, the promise of all its apples and apricots, peaches and pineapples, greengages and goosegogs was not enough to tempt Aberglasney's current owner, Mrs Harries, to remain in residence enjoying the fruits of her inheritance in solitary splendour.[1]

A century and a quarter later, as the seeds of the Aberglasney Restoration Trust began to show signs of germination, the old Kitchen Garden was the part of the Aberglasney complex that presented the blankest canvas (aesthetically, at least) to the restoration team: four plain, somewhat crumbling stone walls and a gently sloping panel of grass and weeds punctuated only by a handful of straggly shrubs that had been bypassed by the ploughing for potatoes of the swinging sixties, and a singular sort of crazed Ben Gunn survivor of the apple-tree race. A solitary apple-tree cousin in the next-door enclosure grimaced an echoing gesture.

An old walled garden no longer stocked with plants is like a dusty deal table, in the echoing kitchen of an empty house, that once was kept scrubbed and that groaned with the quantities of food being prepared for the resident family and its household. It is a familiar story, common to the kitchen gardens of 'big houses' all over Britain. If the property is an important one, with lots of visitors, the kitchen garden can become something useful, like a car park. One in a thousand is actually restored, or continues to function as a productive garden. But very often in places of lesser interest someone

Once again Aberglasney changed hands. Once again the change reflected the rise to power of a new class. . .now it was a fortune made via the Empire that enabled the new owner to acquire landed status.

is given planning permission to build, and The Garden House is put on the map. Here comes the elegiacal note again, but now we can cheerfully suppress it. Something quite unique has happened at Aberglasney. A kind of fairytale is being realized before our eyes. The unwanted kitchen gardens have been granted new leases of life – they find themselves reincarnated. We should perhaps explain that two garden areas (formerly – and formally – functional ones) are bracketed together in this chapter. They are the vast *tabula rasa* of the Upper Walled Garden, plus the more modest and only partly enclosed space of what is to be known as the Kitchen Garden. Once both were purely functional in layout and in aim: they had to furnish provender. Now they enter a new era. They are bound to provide pleasure.

The larger and more exciting of the two enclosures is that Upper Walled Kitchen Garden. It occupies the best part of half an acre. With the most minor of blips (which we shall come to) it really does offer a clean sheet to be filled in any conceivable way. With one of those sleights-of-hand for which Aberglasney is becoming famous, a fairy godmother waved a magic wand and *'PING!'* – one of the most celebrated garden designers appeared on the scene charged with giving this garden space a new life.

Penelope Hobhouse, like Hal Moggridge, was asked to join the Aberglasney team at an early stage as principal design consultant. It is a measure of the gardens' intrinsic power – and of the ambitions of the restoration concept – that one of Britain's most eminent garden designers was drawn into the scheme at its outset, with a brief to create plantings of inspired quality in a layout that would be aesthetically pleasing overall, but specifically to do so using 'choice rather than banal plants' to provide sustained horticultural interest throughout the seasons.[2] It is rare in our day to be able to indulge in the freedom not to reconstruct, re-create or even reinterpret the past, but to make a new garden of delight in a space delineated goodness how long ago. You could see this shadowing of history as elusive, allusive: just enough perhaps to suggest the ghost of an idea. Penelope Hobhouse chose to make a passing reference to the period when Bishop Rudd and his son the baronet owned Aberglasney – the early seventeenth century – as a starting point for the structural elements of her design, so that in a way it is rooted in the past, but then she let her imagination soar in choosing the details of the planting to make the garden inspired and inspirational.

A pause. Suspense. Before we can enjoy some cake we must deal with the bread-and-butter of our History module.

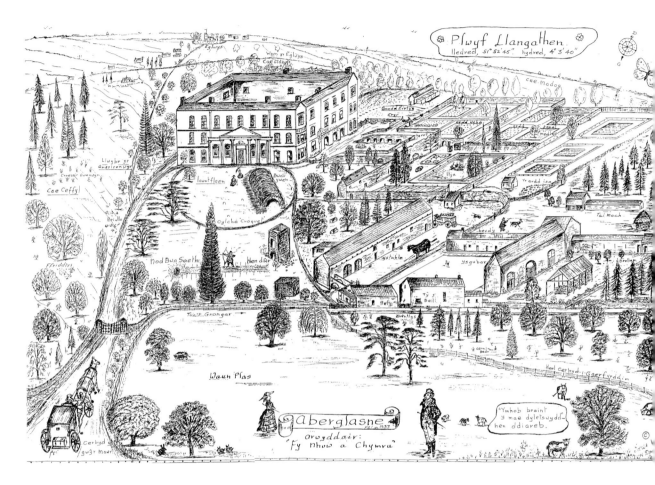

First we need to reel back to the beginning of the nineteenth century. Once again Aberglasney changed hands. Once again the change reflected the rise to power of a new class. The Rudds two centuries before represented wealth derived from the Church; the Dyers a hundred years ago had become rich through the Law; now it was a fortune made via the Empire that enabled the new owner to acquire landed status. In the early 1800s the name of Phillips or Philipps becomes central to the Aberglasney story. The key figure is surgeon Thomas Phillips, and he makes an exotic (if delayed) entrance, arriving from Pembroke by way of India in the company of a married lady who was not his wife – his coming fanfared by arduous preparations by various members of his family. The effort must have been worthwhile. Thomas Phillips lived for twenty years at Aberglasney, but continued to put in appearances a hundred years later, for he is one of the contented ghosts whose spirit is reported to haunt the gardens: we briefly met him (or people who claim to have met him) in Chapter One.

But first, the facts.[3] Young Thomas Phillips went to India in around 1768–70 as a surgeon in the service of the Honourable East India Company. During thirty years there

ABOVE *This bird's-eye vision of the mansion and its surroundings draws on keen childhood memories. As the gardener's son, Idris Davies knew every intricacy of the grounds, garden structures and outbuildings before and during World War Two. Here he depicts the place in its Victorian heyday.*

he became Head Surgeon and amassed an investment of some £25,000 in the Company's funds. In 1799 he wrote to his father telling him of his intention to return home and buy an estate in Carmarthenshire. The three immediate members of what was evidently a close family – his father, also Thomas, by profession a tanner in Pembroke town, his brother John, an attorney of Llandeilo, and his sister Bridget Walters of Perthcereint in Cardiganshire – all set about looking for a likely property.

Aberglasney had just come on the market: 'All that Valuable Capital Mansion and Demesne Land called Aberglasney. . .with several Farms conveniently divided and contiguous to the said Mansion, containing 504 Acres of excellent Arable Meadow and Pasture Land. . .'. The mansion, described as 'Large and Handsome, consists of Four good Rooms on the Ground Floor, with suitable Bed Rooms, and convenient Offices, fit for the Reception of a Large Family, extensive Out Buildings, a Good Garden, and excellent Water at Command.'

Bridget wrote to her brother in India about 'Aberglassnea near the broad oak. . .a sweet place, the situation is delightful. I fancy you must remember it. It belongs to the family of the Dyers. . .'. The brother and sister's familiarity with the area was natural, for the Phillipses had connections with the parish.[4] Bridget described Aberglasney as 'a very hansom mansion' that could not have been built 'for less than £4000'. The estate was worth £500 a year. 'This is worth buying,' she said: you can almost hear the emphasis on each word. Her brother John thought that Aberglasney had 'everything to commend it for the price that is required, 10,000 guineas'. He told Thomas in India, 'It's so desirable a thing that I am anxious you should have it. It will be an immediate residence for any gentleman.' John was clearly conscious of matters of social status – he had now adopted the alternative spelling of Philipps that implied more aristocratic connections – and assured his brother of other desirable aspects of the property. 'At this place we are surrounded by great folks. Perhaps there is not a neighbourhood in England superior to it.' He would have had in mind the superior company at Dynevor and Golden Grove in particular. Aberglasney had cast its spell over a new set of people. Aberglasney was going to play hard to get.

W.H. Dyer had put an asking price of £15,000 on the property, but by June 1801 he had reduced his sights to 10,000 guineas 'in ready money'. John Philipps began to negotiate with Herbert Lloyd, the Carmarthen lawyer who was acting for Dyer. But could the purchase money be transferred from India in time for the following Michaelmas, 29 September 1802? John Philipps hoped to persuade William Paxton or another of his acquaintants to advance the purchase price. Paxton might have been expected to show some fellow-feeling. He had bought the Middleton estate in 1789 with his own fortune from India, and by 1802 the great mansion of 'Asiatic pomp and splendour' designed for him by S.P. Cockerell was being described as 'one of the best built and most magnificent houses in Wales'.[5] The nabob of Middleton did not choose to be magnanimous, and remained reluctant to help when things got really tough later.

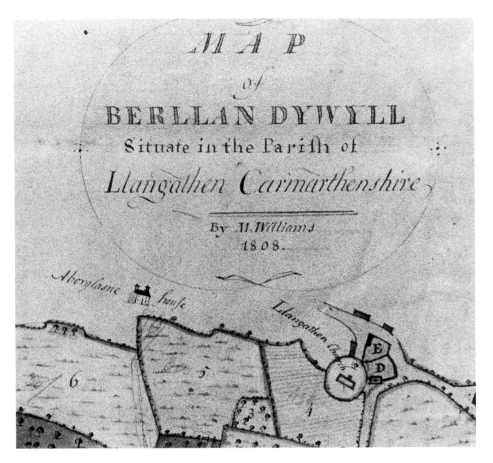

LEFT *The lands of Aberglasney are separated by the Towy river to the south by the farm of Berllandywyll, which formed part of the Cawdor estate of Golden Grove. This map shows the usage of each field on the farm, but 'Aberglasne house' sits in limbo beyond its boundary – the shape of which is quite recognizable today. Note that there is no road below the church: that came later, when Cilsaen bridge was built across the Towy.*

courtyard structures (and perhaps what they were called!), the locations of walls and garden buildings, as well as where the frames and hotbeds were situated.

The improvements made to the property while John Philipps was holding the reins seem to have consisted primarily of attending to the fabric of the buildings: a carpenter was paid £4 19s. 11d. for mending the windows and roof (4000 slates were required, and an ironmonger was paid £20 12s. 11d., for lead); a tiler was paid 12s. for 'stripping the chapel' and a carpenter 15s. 6d. for taking down the chapel 'roof'.

The garden was, of course, not neglected. A gardener, Griffith Williams, and his housekeeper wife were engaged at the combined wage of 20 guineas a year. They and the housemaid, who earned five guineas a year, also had full board, for which an allowance of fourpence a meal was made. The fishpond was repaired and cleaned out, as we saw in Chapter Three. Hotbeds were constructed: Daniel Jabel, smith, charged 6s. 4d. for making plates, handles and bars for them in 1804 (as well as fourpence for mending two spades), and David Davids, glazier, was paid £2 18s. 8d. for providing 'white glass' for an extensive-sounding 44 feet of garden frames. The inventory of garden tools also mentions 'Three light Frames & Glass'. Evidence of what was being grown is scanty, although the presence of the frames and hotbeds implies the cultivation of melons and cucumbers, and the forcing of salads and other crops. Even such hot-country exotics as pineapples, perhaps, to tempt the returning India hands: there was certainly a pinery later, and the technology was already available at the turn of the century. But such structures are unlikely to have been located in either of the kitchen gardens, which were relatively distant from the stableyard and the manure that provided the source of heat.

We shouldn't forget flowers for cutting either. Later on Aberglasney's heiress made several entries in her diary about going out into the garden or the greenhouse 'to get some flowers'. One April day she 'had tea and sat doing Violets for Margaret until dinner'. Who Margaret was and what they were doing with the violets are mysteries – making candied flowers for cake decorations, perhaps?[7]

More mundane crops at Aberglasney included potatoes: Catherine John was paid for three days spent lifting them in November 1805. (Her wage was 6d. per day, and that year she earned 15s. 6d. for various jobs including weeding, gathering stones and collecting acorns and haws. Men gardeners earned twice as much – a shilling a day.) Potatoes were still not grown within the quartered confines of the Kitchen Garden proper. With other bulky, space-consuming crops like pulses and Jerusalem artichokes, potatoes were often relegated to 'the slips' – areas of ground outside the garden walls, or even grown in fields.

The kitchen gardens at Aberglasney were restocked with quantities of fruit trees and bushes obtained from the firm of Miller and Sweet, Nurserymen, Seedsmen & Florists of St Michael's Hill, Bristol – a company also patronized by Lord Cawdor, newly ensconced at neighbouring Golden Grove. Red, white and black currants, and several varieties of raspberry cane, were included in a shipment sent via the *Minerva* in November 1805 ('which hope will arrive safe & please') at a cost of £2 5s. 0d.; cherries, peaches and nectarines were promised to follow, and a special offer was made of 'a fine stock of fine Larch & Scotch Fir if wanted'. Messrs Miller and Sweet's new stock perhaps supplemented productive fruit bushes that still survived from the previous century. In 1742 Robert Archer Dyer had recorded in his Commonplace book a 'Memorandum of ye Disposition of ye Espaliers in ye rod Garden' that is unusually precise as to varieties. Although we cannot be sure where the garden was, it is very likely to have been one of these enclosures. The term 'rod' in this context might refer to an orchard where young trees were trained from slips – or rods – into cordons and espaliers. Dyer's rod garden sounds formally laid out, with walks and a 'terras walk':

As ye go down ye walk on ye left hand when you enter
6 Paradise apples
3 Royal russeting as you go on
3 Golden russeting further
6 Pearmain Apples further
6 Orange Pippin further
6 Non Pareils on ye terras walk

LEFT 'Aberglasney from the North' a watercolour of the early 1800s, when Surgeon Thomas Phillips was the owner. (Is he the top-hatted gentleman to whom the sawyer is touching his brim?) The gatehouse archway has already been embellished with antique mouldings. Already well established, the yew tunnel masks the façade, preventing us from seeing what kind of doorcase the house had in its pre-portico days.

That totals thirty apple trees. It was the French custom to train espaliers against the garden walls, but in Britain they might be planted in open ground and trained along a framework of sticks or wires to make freestanding screens.[8] Equally revealing as we read between the lines of Robert Archer Dyer's note is the importance in the garden of the 'walk', encompassing both noun (path) and verb. We can picture him strolling along beside his apple trees in the garden, and mentally reproducing that activity on paper as he describes their planting positions. A combination of healthy exercise and proprietorial pride comes across from this image. It is echoed in the next century in the 'walks' prescribed by the gardening writers and enjoyed by the characters of fiction.

But all the details recorded by John Philipps's clerks sound as if the priorities were the establishment of a functional garden – fertile (a Mr Morris received £1 10s. at the end of 1805 'for Muck for Aberglasney Garden'), well stocked and weed-free – and there is no evidence of sweeping stylistic changes in the garden layout at the start of the new regime. Ornamental aspects of the garden seem to have been taken for granted.

How were the newcomers from India, their relations and visitors struck by what they found at Aberglasney? Word was spreading about the place (thanks in part to the continuing fame of John Dyer). A friend, Thomas Turner, wrote in 1809 to Thomas Phillips from Red Lion Square, sounding as if he would relish an invitation: 'I hope you have enjoyed your health and your charming grounds. I have heard them spoken of as extremely pleasant – and indeed to read Dyer's Grongar Hill would almost make any one envy its possessor.'[9]

The era when Thomas Phillips and Jane Moore took up residence in Llangathen is one particularly familiar to those of us who are fans of Jane Austen. Through her eyes we can picture members of the family at recreation in the open air. Perhaps, like Mr Collins in *Pride and Prejudice*, for whom 'to work in his garden was one of his most respectable pleasures', the new owner attended to some gardening tasks himself, although perhaps poor health prevented this. Mr Collins's fictional parsonage at Hunsford had a large and well laid out garden and visitors were subjected to a thorough tour: 'Here, leading the way through every walk and cross walk, and scarcely allowing them an interval to utter the praises he asked for, every view was pointed out with a minuteness that left beauty behind.' Aberglasney's superb views towards Grongar Hill would certainly be brought to visitors' attention – no doubt less importunately than by the tiresome Mr Collins; thanks largely to John Dyer's poetry, appreciation of the Picturesque was at its height. Walks and cross walks there must certainly have been in the compartmented gardens at Aberglasney, no doubt considered rather old-fashioned for the period, but not on that account demolished and replaced by the Regency and early Victorian owners. Why not?

One theory for the gardens' survival is that the Phillips/Philipps family was 'anxious to prove their ancient origins and connections... and hence not eager to innovate so as not to appear too *nouveau riche*'.[10] John Philipps the Llandeilo lawyer seems to have been particularly image-conscious. Besides adopting the less common Philipps spelling of the surname, John once expressed concern at the poor quality of the seal his brother Thomas was using in India ('I observe the seal you used with your arms on your letter. . .to be very poorly and imperfectly done') and had a replacement made. In the next generation the Walters Philipps arms, quartered, was displayed in painted glass in the large window above the fine staircase leading upwards from the great hall, with the motto *Fy Nuw a Chymru* – My God and Wales. (Sadly this splendid heraldic window was smashed by vandals during Aberglasney's nadir in the late 1960s.) All this enabled the household to come across as a family of pedigree living in a house with a history. Crumbling 'antiquities' like the gatehouse/folly would just add extra colour.

The coldness that entered the relationship between Thomas and his brother John (who benefited not a jot from the surgeon's munificence) was offset by the warmth of the ties with another branch of the family. Thomas was very close to his sister Bridget, whose persuasive letters, as we saw earlier, had helped determine the purchase of Aberglasney. In about 1780 she had married Abel Walters, who had set out in trade as a tanner but became a successful farmer at the family home of Perthcereint in Cardiganshire, and whose prosperity was augmented when he inherited other properties from a relative. The Walters family held a peripheral position in society: they had some distinguished connections and had married into the gentry, but did not possess an estate whose rental allowed them to live a life of ease. The Phillips family claimed descent from a Middleton of Middleton Hall; the Walters had a drop of the blood of the Vaughans of Golden Grove.[11] Three of Abel and Bridget Walters children survived (though not their eldest son, Thomas). They were John, who becomes central to the Aberglasney story, and his two spinster sisters, Frances and Jane – indomitable ladies, inveterate correspondents who cut their letter-writing teeth in epistles to their Uncle Thomas at Aberglasney. The Aberglasney connection was the making of this family of Walters, who spent a good deal of time waiting on the ageing Thomas Phillips at Aberglasney, 'competing with the faded but very tenacious Mrs Jane Moore'. It brought them both prestige and wealth.[12]

Modernizing changes did take place to the layout of the grounds at Aberglasney under Thomas Phillips's heir. Between the 1827 an unpublished Ordnance Survey draft and

ABOVE *A solitary apple tree, identity unknown, props itself up on an elbow near the doorway to the lower Kitchen Garden. Some improvers see it as an eyesore to be removed, others as a timely reminder of the past in a renovated setting that looks unnaturally pristine. Its saving grace is its treasury of lichens, a hallmark of unpolluted air.*

RIGHT *The Kitchen Garden (seen from the doorway into the Upper Walled Garden) was the first area to begin to look at all ship-shape and garden-like. Dwarf box has been planted around the four timber-edged beds and over the bottom path a new tunnel of crab apples is being trained.*

RIGHT *A veteran apple tree grows slightly off-centre, allowing an uninterrupted sight-line from the lower doorway to its counterpart into the Upper Walled Garden. The spread of the tree canopy, however, coincides nicely with the rondel where the cross-paths meet.*

LEFT AND RIGHT *A squat, square-topped doorway divides the Kitchen Garden from the Stream Garden. While gravel paths are being laid in the Kitchen Garden (left), this dividing wall is still waiting for attention. The 'before' picture (right) with its waist-high weeds shows how much progress has been made here*

Kitchen Garden: path restoration

LEFT *Down alongside the skeletal crab-apple tunnel, the gardeners have set up a bank of cloches to protect cuttings. Some new plant material is being propagated, but included in these nursery beds are cuttings from Aberglasney's most senior citizen, the yew tunnel on the North Lawn.*

RIGHT *Reclaiming the gardens has taken so much clearance, rebuilding and sheer groundwork that plants have seemed low on the list of priorities. At long last the first delivery arrives. Elfyn Rees helps the truck to back into the narrow entrance beside the East Bailiff's Lodge, GHQ of the Aberglasney Restoration Trust.*

The Kitchen Garden: planting begins

LEFT *Gardener Peter Gosling unloads the first contingent of pot-grown plants – a batch of ceanothus. These are intended for the long mixed border designed by Mike Ibbotson to run along the tall, west-facing outer wall of the Upper Walled Garden.*

RIGHT *Almost there: the new plants have reached the Kitchen Garden, but there is a delay before they can be put in. First a supporting framework of wires is to be fixed to the stonework for the climbers and wall-trained shrubs to grow on. Meantime the pots are plunged into a series of planting holes along the pathside that will eventually hold a row of clipped bay trees.*

RIGHT *Peter Gosling rakes the beds to the proverbial fine tilth before sowing them with a crop of green manure. Dug into the ground later in the season, it will fertilize and condition the soil – and meanwhile it discourages weeds from germinating.*

ABOVE AND RIGHT *Gardeners building the new crab-apple tunnel with hazel rods coppiced from Pigeon House Wood. Ayshea Cunniffe-Thomas lends Peter Gosling a hand.*

The Kitchen Garden: preparations

LEFT *The stonework bristles with brand-new vine eyes that will soon be wired to support climbers and wall-trained plants. Before restoration, Aberglasney's walls were surprisingly lacking in hardware indicating such usage in the past.*

BELOW *No ghostly apparition but an oversized maquette by Nigel Hughes for a 2-D sheet-steel sculpture of Bishop Rudd. Its temporary siting against the Victorian thuja dividing us from the Pool Garden adds an anachronistic note.*

its published First Edition of 1831 a new approach to the house appears on the map, sweeping in towards Aberglasney's façade from the north-west after leaving the main road halfway between Lanlash and the main turn-off at Broad Oak. On later maps this becomes a tree-lined avenue. By the 1839 Tithe Map the front garden has a semicircular drive and the inverted C-shape of the house has had its open side (facing the courtyard garden) closed off with a new wing, although the portico has not yet appeared on the façade. It was perhaps being planned: the effect of the alterations shown by the successive maps of this period suggest a sense of aggrandizement in the approach to the house to reflect a consolidation in the status of the inhabitants, and of an owner who was about to be High Sheriff. All these changes belong to the era of John Walters Philipps – who had the new coat of arms drawn up and painted in glass on the stair window – and who inherited Aberglasney on the death of his uncle Thomas Phillips in June 1824.

John Walters, the son of Bridget and Abel Walters, was a lawyer. In 1817 he married Anne Bowen of Waun Ifor, Cardiganshire – a prestigious match. After inheriting Aberglasney in 1824 he became a magistrate. In 1825 he received Royal Licence to take the name of John Walters Philipps. Having acted as deputy to his Aberglasney uncle when in 1813 Thomas Phillips served as High Sheriff of Carmarthenshire, he held that office himself in 1841 (when he paid George Grant Francis of the Carriage and Harness Manufactory, Swansea, £10 for a new pair of armorial banners with silk bullion lace, cord and tassels). In her *Christian Ladies' Pocket-book Almanack* his wife Anne records some more down-to-earth events of this busy year. In February 'Mr P found out for certain that he was the Sheriff'. There were visits to his dying father, and then the funeral. The quarterly assizes took the couple to Carmarthen for a week at a time. 'Returned from Carmarthen quite glad all was over', was the heartfelt comment on 14 July. Meanwhile household management went indefatigably on: 'Brewed 7 winchesters of malt' and 'baked 32pd of flower' were regular entries.

The Walters Philippses had four children: but once again what appears to be the Aberglasney ill-luck took effect and their only son, Thomas, died in infancy. Two of the three daughters – Bridget Jane and Elizabeth Frances – died childless in middle or old age. The middle daughter Mary Anne died early, but not before giving birth to a daughter of her own. She became Mrs Mayhew, whose story will be told in due course.

But we must not forget that in our tour of Aberglasney we are still pacing the walks in the walled Kitchen Garden and Victoria is still on her throne. If it is spring, with the fruit trees in blossom, we might (like William Cobbett) prefer to be here than in other intentionally ornamental parts of the pleasure grounds. The advertisement of 1872 gives a word-picture of its flourishing state; and the OS map of fifteen years later confirms that the traditional quadripartite divisions held firm. The rectangle was crossed by axial paths leading (except in the 'back' wall) to gateways to adjacent garden areas, and paths also ran around the garden. The few straggling box bushes paralleling the southern wall indicated that the paths and beds were once neatly outlined in low clipped edgings.

The change of level as the ground falls away to the south-west means that the eastern, 'back' wall of the Kitchen Garden acts as a retaining wall. A walkway along the top continues the parapet walk round the courtyard garden and provides the opportunity, rare in walled gardens without purpose-built banqueting houses or gazebos, to appreciate the ground plan from an elevated viewpoint. It looks as if this raised walkway appeared between the Tithe Map of 1839 and the OS map of 1886. Before this the garden was a trapezoid shape, but at some point in those years an energetic improving owner built the set of aviaries in the no-man's land filling the angle above it, to the south of the house, and regularized this uphill side of the garden rectangle. (Its angles are still not quite 'right'.) The broad, tunnel-like archway that passes below the walkway and enters the garden in the corner nearest the house must date from that building phase: it is different in style, built of dressed stone rather than the rubble of the other walls, and speaks of solid Victorian respectability. Ladies in crinolines might certainly pass this way.

Back to the present. Nowadays from the raised walkway at the top of the garden you look down on quite a different kind of order. Almost the only thing that the new design has in common with the traditional kitchen garden is the emphasis on strong structure. As Victorian garden writer Jane Loudon pronounced, 'Box edgings are the best for gravel walks.' Between the new box edgings in the Upper Walled Garden you will find not straight lines of worthy, functional vegetables but an exuberance of first-class perennials – sheer luxury. The jewel in Aberglasney's horticultural crown.

The concept behind Penelope Hobhouse's design for this garden is an exciting counterpoint between tradition and novelty. The structural planting has impeccable historical credentials. All the evergreens are plants known to have been grown in Britain before 1600. They are the sort of choice trees and shrubs that Bishop Rudd and his son – had they been keen gardeners – might have sought out to impress visitors with their good taste and up-to-the minute plantsmanship. (Indeed, two of the key species chosen to establish the rhythms of the design are still unusual in British gardens, giving Aberglasney another feather

BELOW *Hidden surprises are always turning up. The higher boundary of the Upper Walled Garden is a retaining wall against the hillside. Contractors repairing the stonework found subsidence at the footings where a spring trickled out of the bedrock. A 'dig' unearthed a dipping pool ornamented with knobbly pieces of waterworn limestone.*

in its cap.) The plants' Mediterranean origins, too, make some allusion to the Italianate inspiration of the Cloister Garden. The layout with its generous ellipses – the oval-in-an-oblong – is loosely inspired by a Robert Smythson plan for Ham House.

Here any 'backward looking' reverential element ends abruptly. It gives way to a dazzling fireworks display of wonderfully anachronistic flowering plants. Past and present are juxtaposed in a virtuoso performance – a contemporary symphony in a period concert hall. 'As soon as it comes to the flowers,' Penelope Hobhouse explains, 'we've just gone for the very best we could think of. There are no restrictions: some of the plants here are herbaceous border classics, but if we want to use a modern cultivar we go for it. We decided it just had to be beautiful.'

Within their framing outlines of box, the perennials are grouped in broad brushstrokes. Varieties are repeated and echoed in the design but without slavish symmetry. The kitchen-garden enthusiast might light upon angelica, cardoon and fennel (a bronze-leaved variety) as symbols of the garden's past culinary incarnation, but they are here for their form's sake alone: their statuesque qualities add height and presence to the central backbone of herbaceous planting.

Penelope Hobhouse has thrown down the gauntlet with this planting plan. It will take an inspired gardener to take up the challenge and make it work – to make and keep it beautiful, and to help it develop over time. She is emphatic that gardening like this with perennials is not a low-upkeep business. They are demanding plants. As they grow their proportions change and the relationship with their neighbours invariably needs adjustment in the longer term. Some may fail and will have to be replaced, perhaps with a different choice of plant. (A nursery area, with 'spares' to replace or infill, is desirable.) Eventually thriving clumps have to be dug up, divided and replanted. There will be chance seedlings – what American gardeners call 'volunteers' – for the gardener to encourage or to sacrifice. But in the short term, too, perennials need weekly or even daily grooming to look their best. Some may need staking, or supporting; the sprawling stems of *Clematis recta* will need to be guided in the right direction and the spent catmint flowers removed to encourage a second flush of flowering. Some plants may need deadheading on aesthetic grounds – or the gardener may choose to leave the

ABOVE *The advertisement that appeared in the* Tenby Observer *of 14 November 1872 gives an eloquent summary of the fine amenities at Aberglasney in its mid-Victorian prime.*

seedheads intact for autumn and winter drama. It is not just green fingers that are called for, but vision.

Caring for the framework plants is more routine, and machinery can help. The structural evergreens need to be clipped to maintain the precise geometry that contrasts so well with the exuberance of the herbaceous planting, wall shrubs need to be tied in and kept in shape, grass mown at different heights according to plan.

The edgings are of box – not the dwarf variety, which might look mean in a design on this sweeping scale, but the species *Buxus sempervirens*. Its bulk is needed to contain and balance the massed herbaceous plants. Nearly 1500 plants delineate the concentric ovals. Pillars of *Phillyrea latifolia* punctuate the beds with vertical accents. It is curious that this classy shrub has always retained it proper botanical name, which comes straight from the Greek. The dictionary weakly offers 'mock privet' and 'jasmine box' as alternatives, but neither ever caught on. Phillyrea it is, and a favourite for topiary all through the Stuart era.

We could weave special local associations around some of the period plants. Portugal laurel, *Prunus lusitanica*, from the Iberian peninsula, might remind us of the Sir John Vaughan of neighbouring Golden Grove, who was among the entourage of Prince Charles when he went a-wooing in Spain in 1623. Mature free-growing specimens of this tree are dotted about the grounds at Aberglasney, and its presence in the Walled Garden makes a symbolic link. Here, though, it is planted architecturally, as living green buttresses around the walls. Along the long lower wall the laurel buttresses are interspersed with the tracery of espaliered morello cherries. The wall that backs on to the Cloister Garden is planted with another old favourite, the quince, *Cydonia oblonga*. This most obdurate of fruits is inedible raw and needs lengthy cooking.

Then we have the mulberries, and a chance to spin a slender yarn that connects James I with the first two generations of Aberglasney Rudds. Grown as tall standards, the trees are grouped in threesomes at the four corners of the plan. In homage to King James these are white mulberries – *Morus alba* – not the source of the succulent drupes of the edible 'black' mulberry, with which garden visitors are often caught red-handed. We are reminded that in 1609 James I determined to establish a British silk industry. He ordained the creation of mulberry gardens at St James's Park and Greenwich Park and had a thousand of these mulberry trees sent to each county town to be sold at six shillings per hundred. One wonders how they were received in Carmarthen. Did the Vaughans of Golden Grove and the Rices of Dynevor compete with the Bishop at Aberglasney to experiment with growing the new tree and accruing royal favour? James's high hopes for a domestic silk industry met with little success. The silkmoth does not thrive in our cold climate, and even the mulberry trees intended as food for its larvae would have found it hard going to become established as Britain's climate entered a colder phase. Today black mulberries are not very common, and white mulberries quite rare in British gardens. Had the story been a happier one for James's ambitions,

Penelope Hobhouse would have had to choose a different tree for her Aberglasney garden plan. Not only would caterpillar-nibbled mulberry foliage present an unsightly picture, but the tree would qualify as Useful rather than Ornamental, and must therefore be ruled out. For the glory of this garden is its sheer indulgence. It is a celebration of the garden as art, not of the craft of gardening.

The Upper Walled Garden presented a blank canvas for a new painting, we thought. Not quite. Two 'anomalies' insinuated their presence into the design. Neither is attention-seeking, neither interferes with the grand plan: you could easily overlook them on a brief visit. They add a subtle gloss of time, like the incidental fleck of a fossil in some sawn stone, or a discreet knot or burr marking smooth polished timber.

The first is a mini water feature. The restoration team was about its task of repairing and repointing the walls, and was approaching the end of this mighty job, when a bit of subsidence was spotted as you approached the far corner – the 'uphill' part of the garden, nearest the church. A little investigative digging showed that here the wall sits on bedrock, and some falling away of the built stones above this was to be expected. More digging revealed some buried stony structures on the garden side. And through the bedrock seeped a gentle spring. Time (once again) to call in the archaeologists. They found a little clay-sealed dipping pool lined with stonework. A neat overflow allowed water to filter out and irrigate the garden soil below. ('I could have told you so,' Idris Jones, the gardener's son might have said; 'We used to grow watercress up here, and catch tadpoles.') Mixed in amongst the working stones were a handful of knobbly pieces of waterworn limestone brought in for sheer decoration.

Date of the feature? Uncertain (a determination that is par for the course here at Aberglasney). The spring, of course, is timeless. Its trapping in a dipping pool may be several centuries old (gardeners have always liked to have a supply of water to hand), but the feature uncovered has Victorian or even Edwardian decorative overtones. Those knobbly rocks crop up a good deal in the watercourses that cut through the carboniferous limestone not far to the south-east of here. A century ago when coal, steel and attendant industries were bringing prosperity and a building boom to towns near here, such curiosities were in demand. Ambitious gardeners incorporated them into their grottoes and rockeries (not, we hope, according to Reginald Farrer's 'Almond-pudding system' where they were stood in a ring like so many misshapen druids at an impromptu *eisteddfod*). Simpler souls incorporated them to surmount their gateposts or as cappings to the walls confining their villa gardens – and you can see them there still, lining the New Roads and Alexandra Terraces and Jubilee Crescents of a dozen upstart townships. Here they are at Aberglasney. Perhaps they were a contribution from the Mayhew era? The knobbly rocks have been labelled 'boboloobies' by the restoration team. Where does the word come from? Another mystery.

The second time-capsule incident in this garden can be found against the opposite

ABOVE *Pride and status radiate from John Walters, who added 'Philipps' to his name when he inherited Aberglasney from his maternal uncle in 1824. Many of Aberglasney's nineteenth-century 'improvements' date from the forty-odd years when he was in possession.*

wall – near the doorway that leads to the lower Kitchen Garden. Here lies – and the verb is deliberately chosen – a collapsed apple tree of as yet unknown identity. The centenarian sprawls along the ground in ungainly fashion – raising its hoary head to drop yet another crop of fruits. The ruthless restorer would long ago have had it cut up (you could hardly say cut down) to give the new garden design a real *tabula rasa*. Aberglasney has mercifully stayed its hand.

What looks at first sight to be a sad relic turns out to be a repository of botanical treasures. A quick survey of the lower stems and branches revealed no fewer than thirty-nine species of lichen and moss (not to mention numerous invertebrates living in the moss tufts). The high lichen diversity indicates an unpolluted, humid, mild climate: these are battle scars to be worn proudly. The apple won't last forever: its days are doubtless numbered. But sparing that tree for a decade or so more will give time for the new apple varieties planted in the lower garden to establish themselves and perhaps to become colonized by some of the lichens from the parent tree. Its more upstanding neighbour in the next-door garden is also host to a score and more of mosses and lichens. Keeping these venerable trees at least for a while provides the bridge through time that may save yet more of Aberglasney's unsung treasures.[13]

There's room here for anomalies and mysteries. When perfectionist American pioneers made their celebrated patchwork quilts, with geometrical patterning repeated with mechanical accuracy, triangles and diamonds dancing in symmetry across the surface, they always introduced some deliberate flaw into their creation, at the last minute, as it were: they inverted the shapes, or suddenly used an unmatching fabric in some border or corner. This sudden flash of humility, the admission of the maker's fallibility, was important, because only God was supposed to achieve perfection.

RIGHT *Once this was the well-ordered kitchen garden, with box-edged gravel paths running round and criss-crossing it. Neglect and crops of potatoes a few decades ago allowed the rank weeds and coarse grasses of disturbed ground to take over. This view from the corner nearest the house shows one of the periodic clearance operations.*

LEFT *The garden slopes down at a gentle gradient and its south-westerly aspect is a favourable one. The wall to the right of the house acts as a retaining wall against the hill, and has a walkway along the top. On the left of the picture is the sole surviving apple tree, a repository of mosses and lichens that thrive in the pure air. Otherwise the space is a blank canvas awaiting Penelope Hobhouse's design.*

The Upper Walled Garden: preparing the canvas

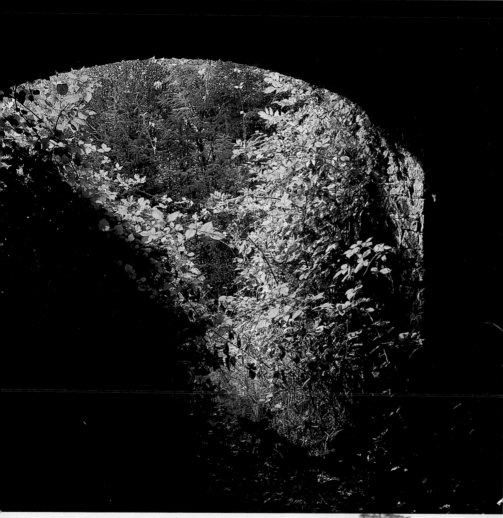

LEFT From the corner of the garden nearest the house a tunnel leading beneath the walkway is broad enough to wheel a barrowload of vegetables through. Conveniently it leads to the side of the house where the kitchens used to be. The outhouses in this area are particularly dilapidated, although their decay is masked by rampant vegetation.

RIGHT The centre of the garden is the ideal place for the continuous bonfires needed to dispose of unwanted timber – dead or diseased trees and shrubs that are being cleared from the woods, and the forests of ivy and other woody colonizers that are being removed from the walls.

RIGHT *The kitchen tunnel is a dank and gloomy place at the best of times. Overhung with laurels and silted up with frequent flooding, it became thoroughly uninviting, although the prospect of the sunlit garden beyond might lure the visitor through.*

LEFT *The old Kitchen Garden's northern wall backs on to the Cloister Garden beside the house. Along its top runs the broad parapet walkway. One or two box bushes have survived in this area, and near the kitchen tunnel a small fig tree clings tenaciously to the mortar into which it has plunged its roots.*

RIGHT *Repairing the parapet walk above the kitchen tunnel. There is a kink in the geometry here but these minor irregularities don't detract from the impression of a series of rectilinear garden compartments.*

Repair work begins on the old Kitchen Garden walls

CHAPTER SIX

The Wood Where Echo Talks

The Twentieth Century:
Rumour, Reality, Restoration

OUR FINAL PART OF THE EXPLORATION of Aberglasney's numberless gardens takes us uphill, beside and behind the mansion, to an amorphous wooded area shaped like an inverted funnel – it qualifies as 'grounds' rather than 'garden' – through which the Glasney in its upper reaches threads its way towards the house. Through it a path lined with pink primroses used to lead towards the church. This is not a well-defined, purposeful, more-or-less regular enclosure like those we visited earlier; nor are the twentieth-century garden stories we hear as distinct even as some of those we came across before. What has been passed down has often been distorted in the telling and in the remembering, so that myth and malice thrive, shading out truth just as the dark laurels and rhododendrons in this thicket drove out native woodland herbs. Chinese whispers about what has happened at Aberglasney since, say, 1900, make a broken chorus calling for the skill of a Dylan Thomas to compose them into some poetic *Milk Wood* shape:

[*Wineglasses tinkling and bottles being smashed*]
FIRST VOICE: Watch, and be sober!
SECOND VOICE: Wouldn't sign the Pledge.
THIRD VOICE: Wouldn't pay the bills. Reckless extravagance!
FOURTH VOICE: By his own hand?
FIFTH VOICE: Drank herself to death!
FINAL VOICE (*decided*): Well I wouldn't go near the place, not at night anyway.
[*Fading: a male voice choir singing spirituals*]

Steady on: this is getting to sound too much like soap opera. But it is hardly exaggeration: there have been real drama and tragedy here within the last few lifespans. The place has changed hands three or four times, in circumstances always attended by some twist of plot that would make respectable fiction. From a healthy, thriving Edwardian estate it has plunged into a nadir of neglect, only to rise again transformed into an entirely new entity. Before we investigate these events, however, let us take brief stock of what we find on terra firma, or rather the slightly muddy leafmould we find beneath our feet.

We are literally in a strange 'neck of the woods' in this chapter, and even the

How do you rescue a neglected wood from its almost impenetrable state of fallen trees, tangled undergrowth, wayward laurels and tracts of mud without losing a certain murky charm?

Americanism is fitting. Once this was known as the American Walk[1]: nothing to do with Aberglasney's colourful wartime visitors, but an inheritance originating from the latter part of the eighteenth century, when the spate of shrub and tree introductions from the New World inspired landscape gardeners such as Humphry Repton to devise special planting schemes to accommodate them. Since many (like kalmias, magnolias and rhododendrons) were ericaceous, special peat beds were sometimes created for them. By the mid-nineteenth century, when it is likely that many of the ornamental woody plants here were planted, the proportion of American natives in an American Garden was often quite dilute, but the name remained fashionable. Its presence at Aberglasney is a reminder that the place once had high horticultural pretensions. This dark woodland stands in good contrast to its counterpart at the other end of the property, Pigeon House Wood. That is light, deciduous, semi-natural (in the sense that its predominantly native tree population is a plausible imitation of native woodlands). It has a high canopy and a spacious dignity. This is alien, naturalized – and alluring.

Tackling this area of the garden poses the Restoration Trust with several questions. Do you keep an historic name that is no longer appropriate? How do you rescue a neglected wood from its almost impenetrable state of fallen trees, tangled undergrowth, wayward laurels and tracts of mud without losing a certain murky charm? (Answer: chainsaws and choice plants.) And what do you do when the very purpose of the garden, as a short-cut through-route, is terminated by an elephant-high deer-fence? Beyond the garden an uphill public right of way through a field links the top of this garden with the churchyard. With the area turned into a closed circuit, the landscape consultants meet the challenge of making the dead-end area attractive enough with planting, bridges, pools and come-hither disappearing paths to invite exploration. If only the logistics of property management (an exit-only turnstile, perhaps?) allowed visitors to use the old primrose path to reach the church. That last steep climb to Llangathen church, with its views and treasures, would make a perfect climax to a visit: a chance to see the resting place of so many of the characters we have encountered in these pages.

Enough of the vegetable world. Let's get back to the practicalities, that is to say (as it's Aberglasney), the mysteries. Two particular non-natural features are worth remarking in this area. Right in the dog-leg angle of the lower wood that points to the south-east

Grongar Hill

you may find a slight mound of earth, a tump so inconspicuous in the uneven rising ground you could easily overlook it. Obviously it is manmade, but is it a Mount, or a molehill? Either it was built as a 'feature', or it arose as a spoil heap or rubbish dump. Optimists hope that it will turn out to be something wonderfully Historical and Auspicious, perhaps even contemporaneous with the Italianate raised terraces and walks (such as we find in the Cloister Garden). Its positioning in this important hingepoint corner of the estate tends towards that argument. From early Tudor times artificial hillocks or mounts were deliberately created to afford a viewpoint over the countryside beyond the garden walls (a device more vital in level terrain than in this undulating landscape), though ours is a simple pimple compared to elaborate structures like that built at Hampton Court, which sheltered grottoes and supported spiralling stairways to climb them. (In his essay 'Of Gardens', Francis Bacon envisaged a mount thirty feet high; a bunny could reach the top of Aberglasney's little tump in two bounds.) Mounts appear in gardens through into the eighteenth century: the landscape architect Charles Bridgeman was still incorporating them in his plans at the time when

ABOVE *Through John Dyer's poem of that name, Grongar Hill was once known 'wherever the English language is read'. With James Thomson's* The Seasons, *it helped inspire the appreciation of natural landscape that became the Picturesque movement. From 1800 on, it drew numbers of aesthetes and tourists to the Towy valley.*

RIGHT *The view towards Grongar Hill from Llangathen parish church is not far out of alignment with the view from the Mount in Aberglasney's garden. From Aberglasney (out of sight in the dip to the right of this picture) you are almost in calling distance of the hill, and some people suggest that Dyer's poetic allusion to Echo might be taken literally. The low console-shaped tombstone to the right of centre marks the grave of Colonel and Mrs Mayhew.*

Robert Dyer was streamlining the façade of Aberglasney Mansion and his brother John was steaming up Grongar Hill. Archaeology may one day tell us the story of ours.

The Mount offers a slight vantage point over the ancient, deeply marked boundary between Aberglasney and the neighbouring farm of Berllandywyll, and a prospect up to where the church makes an eye-catcher. But it is in the Grongar direction that visitors might like to experiment with a theory voiced by more than one lad who has grown up in the neighbourhood.[2] It is that John Dyer's injunction in his poem 'The Country Walk' to 'See her woods, where Echo talks' might be taken literally. Now is our chance to find out if Dyer's Echo is more than a poetic conceit. In his poetry if not in any other way John Dyer seems a presence at Aberglasney: we noted earlier that Dyer for the first time in poetry 'gives us a real hill'. He loved the music of the place, he had been a boy here, and he might very well have experimented with the echo as well. Why don't we?

Our Mount may just be the result of ditch-clearing or spoil-dumping; it may once have been higher and more evenly shaped. At any rate it is unlikely to have been a Victorian creation, like a good deal of this part of Aberglasney. It is probably older, or accidental. The second manmade feature we distinguished should be a lot easier to date: the aviary is clearly a building of nineteenth-century vintage. Once again in the absence of evidence we have to look at who owned and was resident in the property to see who might have constructed it.

The fortunes of Aberglasney as it succumbed to vagaries of family history in the last three decades of the nineteenth century are as tricky to follow as are those family fluctuations themselves. The marks made on his estate by John Walters Philipps – High Sheriff, *paterfamilias*, improver – are the predictable ones of someone of his status, as we saw in the previous chapters: he increased the presence and impact of Aberglasney mansion by planting an avenue, erecting a portico, throwing out a bay, and (probably) bringing the gardens bang up to date with the latest horticultural innovations. After he died, though, Aberglasney was for seventy-five years in the hands of a succession of three childless married women. The presence of his daughters on the Aberglasney stage has the two-dimensionality of those cardboard cutout figures in a toy theatre whose movements are governed by sliding rods from the side. We occasionally detect our heroines making some movement across the stage (but since in our case the sound seems to be turned off, or the script missing, their actions offer precious little elucidation to our thickening plot). The mansion also seems periodically to have been let out.

Detectives needed! We would need to find documentary evidence of some kind, or to be able to allocate precise dates to some of Aberglasney's pieces of later Victoriana, to succeed in pinpointing what part (if any) each of these successive incumbents played. An absentee family, or an owner whose heart is not in the job, will keep up the fabric of a house, employ efficient staff and gardeners, put a good face on interior and exterior soft furnishings (wallpaper, upholstery, bedding plants, clipped topiary). But it takes a resident enthusiast to build an aviary or to plant particularly recherché specimen trees – just as sometime in the sixteenth or seventeenth centuries (it now seems) it took the exceptional vision of some kind of Renaissance Man to give Aberglasney its Cloister Garden.

Who was it that built the elaborate suite of six brick-and-wire enclosures to the side of the house, for instance? Received wisdom – in the form of living witnesses who live locally – asserts categorically that these buildings were kennels. Informed sources call them aviaries, perhaps part of a menagerie. Both identifications seem to be correct, as we shall see. What the storyteller yearns to know is the identity of that bird fancier who was keen (and wealthy) enough to indulge this exotic taste. Perhaps it was a tradition at Aberglasney. Did Thomas Phillips and Jane Moore indulge their yearning for the fauna they remembered from the Indian subcontinent? If so the structures would have to date from before the 1820s. Or did they transmit such an interest to their Walters Philipps heirs in the next generations? (Some researcher with several years and boundless patience to spare might comb the correspondence of the spinster sisters Jane and Frances Walters with their rich Uncle Thomas – and with countless others – in

RIGHT *Someone at Aberglasney in the nineteenth century was a keen tree fancier. The cut-leaved oak* QUERCUS ROBUR *'Fennessii', raised in Ireland in the 1820s, is a great rarity.*

search of passing references to matters ornithological.) And what exotic fowl did they fancy?

The nineteenth-century function of the buildings was to house birds, but dogs were indeed kennelled in these enclosures in the twentieth century, within living memory. The answer is both aviary and kennel. Is this how Aberglasney mythology works? Opposing theories are put forward, contradicted, denied; in the end both turn out to contain some truth.

Then there is the wider plant interest of the gardens – largely confined now to a selection of handsome trees that are either exotics or unusual variants of native species, since few shrubs and herbaceous plants have survived the combined onslaught of prolonged neglect and radical renovation. But who was the keen dendrologist who planted handsome rarities like the cut-leaved oak *Quercus robur* 'Fennessii'? One of the handful of notable tree hybrids to come out of Ireland – quirky and individualistic in its impact, the opposite of the biddable building-block accents made by fastigiate Irish yew – this was raised by Fennessey & Son of Waterford in 1820. It takes a connoisseur to choose a tree of such pedigree. Mayhew had Irish connections: perhaps it was his sentimental choice. When was it planted? History holds us in thrall – we would have to cut down the tree and count its rings before we could answer that question.

It is just possible that one of the three Misses Walters Philipps (or, in due course, their respective husbands) kept rare birds or planted rare trees. We must now despatch this group in quick thumbnail sketches. (They will be brief: we have little to tell.) By the time Bridget, the eldest daughter, inherited the estate from her father, she was already separated from her husband. Social life went on. We occasionally meet her chaperoning her niece, the future Mrs Mayhew, at the Llandeilo archery contests, for example. And there was entertaining. Hermione Jennings at Gellideg, a near contemporary of Mary Anne's, visited in August 1866 for a croquet party and dance hosted by 'Mother Gamp, alias Mrs Harries'. Hermione described Aberglasney as 'a curious old-fashioned looking place' but appreciated the 'elegant cold collation' served in a small room beyond the drawing-room. They played croquet on the lawn all afternoon, there were twenty-four for dinner, and afterwards they had 'dancing in the hall, which was oak, but we were obliged to dance around the billiard table which was too heavy to be moved'.[3]

Though Mrs Harries is described as 'in residence' in 1872, in the same year the *Tenby*

Observer was offering it as a desirable property to let, as we saw in Chapter Five. On her death in 1881 Mrs Harries' surviving sister Lizzie inherited the rental of Aberglasney for her lifetime, but she seems to have spent most of her time either at the neighbouring house of Hafod Neddyn, which her father had bought in a property-buying spree in the 1850s, or at her husband's home at Pentypark in Pembrokeshire.[4] Aberglasney was certainly let out in 1892, when the Cambrian Archaeological Association made its excursion to the area in August of that year. Its members were 'hospitably entertained by Mr Lewis-Lewis of Swansea who is at present residing at Aberglasney'.[5] When Aunt Lizzie died childless in 1900, the estate went to the daughter of the middle sister, Mary Anne, who had died when her child was barely two. That niece – another Mary Anne – was the only representative of the next generation.

It is the name of Mayhew that clearly dominates the district in the first half of the twentieth century. The Mayhews lived at Aberglasney for a surprisingly brief spell, and then *in absentia* exercised an even more profound influence for nearly half a century – it is almost as if they laid a dead hand on the place.

Mrs Mayhew inherited in 1900. This important lady is hardly more in focus than her shadowy aunts, in part perhaps because much of her childhood was spent with her father and stepmother at Bwlchbychan in Cardiganshire. We encountered her briefly on the archery ground in Chapter One, but the image of that lively, talented girl with an appetite for strawberries is quickly absorbed into the anonymity of the respectable married woman. Miss Mary Anne Emily Jane Pryse (variously called Mary, Molly, Marianne or even Emily, as well as Miss Pugh Pryse) at the age of twenty-three married Lieutenant Charles George Adams Mayhew of the 23rd Royal Welch Fusiliers on 12 December 1872. She must have been quite a catch. An undated letter tucked into an album belonging to her aunt Bridget implies the young woman was in demand: 'Is it true that Marianne has just refused Capt Bowen? So a little bird has whispered to me,' wrote the unidentified correspondent from the Reform Club, one Thursday.[6] That September a friend (the signature is illegible) wrote to the bride-to-be expressing surprise and pleasure at the news of the engagement to Mayhew, having 'heard nothing except that there was a flirtation going on'.[7] From this letter we learn little more of Lieutenant Mayhew's character than that 'he seem[ed] very nice'. Another cardboard cutout. Even his family background remains in the shadows: the handful of facts we have includes that his father was Charles Mayhew of Chester Terrace, Regent's Park, and that young Charlie was educated at Eton. He was not an only child: in 1886 we find him paying his brother Walter's debts and his one-way passage to Australia – a black sheep being sent where he might safely graze, out of harm's way, it seems.[8]

The Mayhews' marriage seems to have been happy enough, but it was childless. Military duties kept the couple apart for prolonged periods and generated bouts of regular correspondence, when Charlie Mayhew addressed his wife as 'My own darling

Beedie' and signed himself 'Your own Boo'. The Beedie–Boo endearments persist through over twenty-five years of married life, although the content of the letters dwindles from lengthy outpourings of affection to brief reports of arriving safely and minor alarms about having forgotten to pack a sponge-bag. Much of their married life was passed in Derbyshire, where he was serving.[9] There was a flurry of excitement in the 1880s when he was sent to India with the Royal Welch Fusiliers to take part in the Anglo-Burmese War ('which, however, had reached a termination before he reached the country'). His obituary none the less credited the Colonel with 'a distinguished military career'.

The Mayhews seem to have taken up residence at Aberglasney in 1902 and set about living an everyday life of country-house folk. Repairs and improvements were made to the property. Braces of pheasant were despatched to their friends. The middle-aged couple looked set for a good few years in their new home. The thirty servants they employed included coachmen, groundsmen, masons, gardeners and carpenters, with butlers, cooks, parlour maids and ladies' maids indoors.[10]

Colonel Mayhew made an indelible impression. He gave eloquent speeches, turned antiquarian to investigate the history of his new home and learned Welsh. He is best remembered for his ardent addiction to Temperance. The Mayhews' virulent teetotalism did not simply extend to banishing alcohol from the village but even to banishing those tenants who declined to sign the Pledge.

Colonel Mayhew was President of the Llangathen and District Temperance and Band of Hope Union. The handsome Temperance Hall erected in the field above the house, on the 'new road' to Cilsaen bridge was built entirely at Mrs Mayhew's expense in mock-Tudor style by one Allcard, a master builder from Sheffield.[11] Slogans around the twin towers in letters clearly visible from some distance enjoined the passer-by, in Welsh and in English, to '. . .watch and be sober. . .'. It's easy nowadays to giggle or groan about the Mayhews' *idée fixe* of sobriety, but their building a hall for the community was a piece of broader philanthropy, and if the pledge was taken with a pinch of salt by some, the gesture was appreciated by many. Besides providing a focus for Band of Hope activities and the like, the building served as a village hall. Later it hosted less obviously 'dry' gatherings – it was turned into a NAAFI, with a bar for the soldiers, during World War Two.

A number of colourful stories in circulation illustrate Colonel Mayhew's aversion to alcohol. He is supposed to have closed down the pubs on the estate, but the Three Compasses had already been transformed into Church House before his day.[12] It is said that on arriving at Aberglasney he threw out the entire contents of the winecellar. Maybe bottles were emptied straight into the stream that ran through the cellar and was formerly used to cool the wine: a 'large quantity of empty bottles' was noted in the cellar in 1940.[13] Others say bottles were thrown into the fishpond. In the mid-1970s, when David Charles owned Aberglasney, two unopened bottles are reported to have

been found, one of wine and one of brandy.[14] One wag commented that in view of the myths about Aberglasney's monastic past they were probably Blue Nun and Benedictine. When in the 1940s the new owners Mr and Mrs Eric Evans found a nineteenth-century inventory of the winecellar among the papers at Aberglasney they realized the extent of what they had lost.[15]

Colonel Mayhew has set up his own aura of myth, in counterbalance perhaps to those he helped to perpetuate of Aberglasney's past, such as the presence of a monastery on the spot. Of one thing we can be sure: the gardens were kept in good order under the military precision of the Mayhews. Topiary, lawn edgings, gravel paths and bedding had to look spick and span when bazaars and rallies were held in the grounds, and Mrs Mayhew will have expected top-class produce to serve at her dinner parties. Some people think the Colonel was responsible for planting some of the more interesting trees around the place, a commendable trait, you might think, in a garden. However, 'They all seem to be of weeping habit,' someone said; 'He seems to have been

ABOVE *Postwar tranquillity. Time has swept away both Nissen huts and Victorian bedding schemes. Eric Evans and his young family own the estate and skies are blue. The house, however, remains rather a handful. The sketch is signed 'P.R. Sept. 1949' and is by Mrs Evans' brother, Peter Rogers.*

156

a miserable kind of bloke.' The myth is further embellished and embroidered.

The idyll of trees, temperance and other good works came to an abrupt end with Colonel Mayhew's sudden death on 26 October 1907. The death certificate gave the cause of death as 'acute pyaemia' (septicaemia). An obituary notice gave the cause of death as a chill, 'first contracted at his last public appearance. . .at Huddersfield, where he had gone to represent the Diocese of St David's on the General Society of the Church of England Temperance Society'. It seems temperance was the death of him. He was buried at Llangathen on 29 October. The Bishop of St David's came to his funeral and signed the church register. We note these details because they are the official version of what happened. They are contradicted by a sporadic rumour that he took his own life and that the gentry closed ranks to conceal the suicide. The storyteller has been unable to trace the origins of this notion.

Colonel Mayhew's burial merited the attendance of the bishop but has not continued to attract much notice. The tomb he shares with his wife a stone's throw in the Aberglasney direction from the church tower is console-shaped, the delicate carving decorating its scrolled sides now coloured by lichens. Its surround is not in pristine condition, perhaps a sign of its initial occupant 'turning in his grave'. The quantities of alcohol that have subsequently flowed at Aberglasney might well have had that proverbial effect on our abstemious colonel.

After Colonel Mayhew died, for the passage of a generation Aberglasney enters a strange kind of limbo. Some months after his death something seems to have snapped in the mind of the widowed Mrs Mayhew, who (it is said) quite abruptly upped and left. Oddly specific anecdotes attend the circumstances of her sudden departure. She is said to have left behind all her clothes, and her shoes 'with mud all over them', and 'all the taps running'. A cousin coolly contradicts such minutiae: 'Mrs Mayhew was not the sort of person who turned on taps. She'd have had people to do that kind of thing for her.' Before leaving she had, however, been sufficiently level-headed to organize a sale of 'Surplus Household Appointments', with a forty-odd page catalogue 'rich in items of furniture from the Chippendale and Sheraton periods', in old Welsh oak and pieces reputed to have belonged to 'the Poet Dyer', as well as pictures, books, plate and linen. The sale on 1st–3rd April 1908 raised some £2200.[16] By 1909 she was living at the Norfolk Hotel, South Kensington, where the Mayhews had often stayed when in London. She was there for the next thirty years.

It is not unusual for grief to cause the bereaved partner to break down in some way. An inexperienced widow will often feel unable to cope with the management of a property whose affairs her husband has always handled, but this was not the case here. Nevertheless there was something bizarre in Mrs Mayhew's flight and subsequent obliviousness. She wilfully neglected the financial business of her properties, allowing insurances to lapse, refusing to answer letters and allowing bills, rates and wages to go unpaid. The reliable tenants at her Bwlchbychan house asked for some modest repairs to be done and were summarily given notice. One relative feared that the value of the properties would deteriorate – a particularly difficult situation since Widow Mayhew had embarked on a positive spending spree and was running up bills beyond her means. 'I have heard that her purchases of clothes can only be described as reckless extravagance as on getting them home she often does not like them and without being worn they are cast aside and others bought. . .' was one anxiety expressed by an unnamed letter-writer, concerned that his daughters, who stood to benefit from the estate on Mrs Mayhew's death, would end up with nothing.[17]

Mrs Mayhew was determined to be elusive: 'apparently nobody can get to even see her unless meeting her by chance in the street'. A rich widow who had become a loose cannon was a great worry to concerned parties. Was it safe for Mrs Mayhew to go out by herself. What was she doing? Spending income of whose provenance she was not taking due care. Independent and irresponsible – and free – at last? 'I have never known much of her affairs as she always even after her husband's death preferred to manage things herself. . .' wrote the unnamed correspondent; 'From my knowledge of Mrs Mayhew in the past I am perfectly certain she would not agree to have a companion, and even less to a doctor as she always had a rooted objection to the latter'. Maybe Mrs Mayhew was enjoying herself at last – a merry widow. Maybe she was having a mid-life crisis. Maybe she'd taken to drink. Perhaps someone would like to follow up this enigma: this is the province of the novelist, or the earnest research student-cum-trainee detective (there are bills aplenty to study and footwork to be done).

The sad fact is that she largely ignored her responsibilities at Aberglasney, and Aberglasney and its tenants suffered. Periodically some remedial work was done. Occasionally the servants were ordered to get the house ready for her return. Evidence of one such instance gives us a rare glimpse of the gardens. Joseph Hallett, head gardener, recorded that 'Since the Mansion has been done up in 1923' he had been granted '2 men extra in and about the gardens & a Maid to clean the Mansion'. Later, in 1934, Hallett is found costing out the price of asparagus crowns: two-year-old plants were 17/6 and one-year-olds ten shillings per hundred; 'I have measured the bed & I find that it will take about 168 plants.'[18] Whether the project went ahead is unknown, but that it was even under consideration is itself interesting. The investment of time and money involved in creating a new asparagus bed implies that posh company was expected, and that potential asparagus-eaters were somewhere on the scene, or perhaps that a marketable crop was being considered. But Mrs Mayhew never came back.

Aberglasney's principal guardian angel during the interregnum was the famous 'Dame Margaret' – Mrs J.C.V. Pryse-Rice of Llwynybrain.[19] This formidable lady would appear riding sidesaddle, in her smart Edwardian habit, to check up on the state of things at Aberglasney. Another cameo shows her – this time horseless – brandishing her gold cigarette holder with its French cigarette. She assumed the role of custodian to protect the family interest: the substantial properties of Aberglasney and Bwlchbychan in Cardiganshire were to pass through her husband and their eldest daughter Margaret to her grandson. We'll follow the detail of this inheritance through presently. She was evidently a no-nonsense character: she had been made a dame for services to the Red Cross during World War One (her daughter's husband won a VC at Passchendaele), so sorting out Aberglasney was small beer. The residents of Church House were surprised one Sunday evening when the front door opened, a lady walked in and dropped something in a drawer. She explained that she was on her way to church and wanted to leave her keys. 'We hardly knew her, and she didn't even knock. I was a bit startled but my mother explained that she was the landlord,' remembers David Thomas Rees. That was how things were: very upstairs–downstairs.

Mrs Mayhew died intestate in December 1939 at the age of ninety but the question of who was to inherit Aberglasney had already provoked controversy. There were rumours of a lost will. In January 1938 some claimants called Falconer, deciding that possession was nine-tenths of the law, ensconced themselves at Aberglasney. Somehow Dame Margaret heard about this. Major Bishop, agent for the Dynevor estate – who kept an occasional eye on Aberglasney – sped to the mansion. The intruders were abed. Major Bishop knocked on the door and told the inmates to 'leave right away'. A voice protested, 'Don't come in; we've just got into bed and I've got practically nothing on.' 'Madam,' responded the Major, 'I've seen far more beautiful people than you with far less on.' The eviction was successful: the interlopers fled.[20] Solicitor William Wilding Jones and Dame Margaret continued a furious correspondence 'about the Falconers and their atrocious behaviour'. When Mrs Mayhew was told that the Falconers were 'making themselves nuisances', her forthright reply from the Norfolk Hotel was 'I authorize you to deal with the person Falconer.'[21] At nearly ninety, Mrs Mayhew still had at least some of her wits about her, although she chose not to exert them in clarifying who was to inherit her possessions.

A draft will made by Mrs Mayhew around 1900 had indicated that she had thought of leaving considerable amounts of her property including the Aberglasney estate to someone called Stella Collins, the daughter of William and Margaret Collins. Steps were taken after Mrs Mayhew's death to trace any Collins descendants, but all were dead.[22] In the end it was decided that the next of kin were the descendants of the second marriage of Mrs Mayhew's father to Decima Dorothea Rice of Llwynybrain. In 1940 these were two men, George Carbery Pryse-Rice of Llwynybrain and his nephew Eric Evans of Lovesgrove, Cardiganshire, born in 1920 and thus still a minor.[23] The extensive property was divided between them.

The new heir's father and trustee, Brigadier-General Evans VC CB CMG DSO, hero of the First World War, gives us a tenuous continuity link to our next topic: Aberglasney in wartime 1939–45. Shades of the *Boy's Own Paper* enter the next phase of

RIGHT *Surreal skeletal structures emerged from tangled undergrowth in the woods above the Upper Walled Garden. Stout metal wires made a cage-like grid at the front. Animals were implied. 'Kennels,' a local man said. 'They used to keep dogs up here.' 'Aviaries,' said someone else.*

RIGHT *With the tangle of brambles and ivy removed, it became possible to inspect the design of the six enclosures more closely. An aviculturalist who viewed the building* *after the clearance gave the opinion that the cages were meant to house ornamental pheasants, fashionable exotics imported by fanciers, possibly from about 1860 to 1890.*

ABOVE *Spacious shelters made of cream-coloured brick and roofed with slate backed the flight cages to make quite a substantial and sophisticated building.*

RIGHT *Looking southwards along the walkway above the Walled Garden it is hard at first to see just how many separate units might have been hidden under the rampant vegetation.*

The aviary and dog kennels

The American Wood

Aberglasney's history. People who grew up in the area – especially the little boys – come up with little strip-cartoon sequences of memory. Requisitioning, troop occupation and the impingement of World War Two brought unheard-of excitement to their lives. Soldiers vastly outnumbered the civilian occupants of the small village of Llangathen. In the long term it was the people rather than the place that the war changed.

Just once the war came close to home in the form of a bomb, one of three dropped in a line *en route* to Swansea during the punitive raids of 1941. William Rees of Church House and the vicar, in their capacity as Local Defence Volunteers, were guarding the telephone kiosk at Broad Oak when they saw it fall in a field about halfway between Lanlash and Aberglasney. The village boys came down to inspect the crater with awe. Swansea had been smashed; Llangathen parish bore its own small scar.[24]

The Aberglasney property was requisitioned in 1940. Officers under CO Captain Finch lived in the mansion: their mess in the downstairs drawing room gave out on to the loggia overlooking the Cloister Garden. For Other Ranks huts with concrete floors were erected on the lawns in front of the house (turf was removed from beneath the big cedar tree on the front lawn for two of them) and in Cae Ceffyl, the field below the Temperance Hall.[25] A few tree roots were cut when concrete foundations were being laid; the odd land drain was damaged, and obviously new services and pipelines crisscrossed the site. After the war when the military structures were removed and the lawns made good Aberglasney seemed remarkably untouched. (Only the archaeologists attempting to decipher the layers of Aberglasney's hidden past might beg to differ as they encounter yet further subterranean disruptions.) No one remembers the usual commitment to 'Dig for Victory' manifesting itself in the estate's productive gardens. Up the road at Dynevor they were camouflage-painting the famous white cattle lest the wily German bombers recognized the rare breed and used the hapless animals to help them navigate their bombing run towards the steelworks at Llanelli (never mind the castles and landmarks that could not be disguised, nor the tell-tale meanders of the Towy to be read as fluent script directing all comers towards its unmistakeable estuary: the cows could be the give-away). Aberglasney made no such bold strategic moves.

Of all the stirring martial roles in which history might have cast it to play, it was Aberglasney's destiny to wash the dirty linen of the Western Command, and the RAOC brought with them the wherewithal to do this on a grand scale. Mobile Laundry No. 31 Unit Royal Army Ordance Corps was sited in the quadrangle near the stables and cottages. Water was pumped up from the river Towy by means of an engine and pump in a zinc shed near the cottage called the Wern. Electricity was generated on site by big mobile trailers. Mobile Laundry No. 3 Unit, many of its men from the Manchester area, took their place in December 1942. 'Army lorries were back and forth all the time.' Sometimes there were manoeuvres, with lorries racing around the village in 'an alert'.

Sentries posted at the main entrance and near the lodge challenged everyone who passed along the road, including local people walking home from the bus-stop at Broad Oak. The children took to playing soldiers. David Thomas Rees, the eldest, marched his little troop of half-a-dozen boys around, wielding sticks as guns, building huts, imitating the lorries as they drove about the camp – and startling passing womenfolk with sudden piping sentry-challenges of 'Halt! Who goes there?'

Sometime in early 1943 the mobile laundries moved off to North Africa: a promised showing of *How Green Was My Valley* in the Temperance Hall had to be cancelled as a result. The order to move came in the early hours of the morning and some bleary-eyed driver caught one of the pillars a violent blow with his truck as he swung the vehicle past the portico. The damage looked serious: witnessing the encounter as they sped away, Sergeant Fred Wisehall thought the portico might very well collapse. It didn't: when he revisited twenty years later to show his young son the place where he had spent a particularly happy period of his life, there it was as good as new. Behind it the house was now crumbling, but the portico stood firm – thanks to lashings of cement applied to the damaged pillar by the boys the vacating troops left behind.[26]

The RAOC launderers were succeeded by detachments of black American troops. Local people recall the sheer informality of the newcomers. 'Got any gum, chum?' was often met with 'Got any older sisters, kid?' From the start of the war successive batches of stationed soldiers dated local girls, while visiting servicemen's wives were put up by local families. There were occasional tensions, as when hens' laying went down unexpectedly (boys from Llandeilo were found to be stealing the eggs and selling them to American troops) and sometimes hens themselves went AWOL. Such incidents were countered by cases of sheer kindness. Mrs Rees, a St John's Ambulance captain, noticed that something was wrong with one of the village boys whose broken arm was in plaster – his hand looked black. An American medical orderly took a quick look and said 'Yes! Hospital for you!' 'He got a jeep immediately and took the boy to Carmarthen, where they replaced the plaster cast. That was the informality of the Americans for you – not a lot of red tape!', commented Mrs Rees's son David. Then there was their generosity. When the troops came to church services they thought nothing of putting pound notes and ten-shilling notes on the offertory plate: the sidesmen had to put his hand over the notes to stop them falling off. This at a time when a two-shilling piece would be a large amount for the collection, and pennies and sixpences were routine. One time the vicar invited the Americans to organize a special service where they sang spirituals. The old church rang to the strains of 'Joshua fit the Battle of Jericho' and 'By the Rivers of Babylon', while whooped 'A-men's' and 'Glory Halleluja's echoed around the sober, respectable tombs and monuments of Thomases, Rudds and Dyers, Phillipses and Walters Philippses, and generations of Llangathen folk.

More memorable for most minds than the Llangathen bomb was the appearance at Aberglasney of a first-hand link with the Brown Bomber in the burly shape of Top Sergeant Dawson of the United States Army Corps – 'an awesome sight running along the narrow lanes of Llangathen at dawn'.[27] Dawson was the official sparring partner of that Brown Bomber – Joe Louis, from Lexington, Alabama, one of the greatest and most colourful boxers of his day. He took the title of World Heavyweight Champion from James Braddock on 22 June 1937 and reigned for a record twelve years, defending it twenty-five times until 1949, when he retired. The name and fame of Joe Louis was particularly familiar in Wales because the wiry little Welsh boxer Tommy Farr had almost succeeded in beating him in 1937: some thought that Farr should have won the contest. Both Louis and Farr were legends to Welsh schoolboys: Top Sergeant Dawson was up there amongst them.

While the war was still on and Americans still on the scene a new and sadly brief epoch in Aberglasney's history began. In 1945 the young heir Griffith Eric Carbery Vaughan Evans and his bride Barbara Rogers came to take possession of their inheritance.

Enter Mr and Mrs Eric Evans, the happy result of a wartime romance, the encounter played offstage. It was the Queen's Hotel, Westcliffe-on-Sea. Earlier that day on the quarter-deck a good-looking Wren standing smartly to attention had spotted the particularly attractive young lieutenant of the Black Watch who was leading the parade. He too had noticed her. That night on the dance floor 'This gorgeous creature came up and asked me to dance'. Love at first sight? A few months later, in August 1943, they were married. As the war ended they moved to Aberglasney, to live at first in one of the bailiff's cottages. The area was familiar to the eighteen-year-old bride. Not long before, Barbara Rogers's school had been evacuated to Tregib, near Llandovery. 'People joked that I'd climbed over the school wall and come straight here,' she said.

It must have been a time of great hope and promise for people on the estate. Peace had broken out; Aberglasney was in the hands of a young family. Tenants still came up to the big house to pay their rents twice a year, but the business was done in a more informal atmosphere than of old. The war had broken down many stuffy conventions.

The new incumbents had to sift through an Aladdin's caves of barns and cottages where furniture and china had been packed up during the wartime occupation. In the house itself Eric Evans made magical finds beneath the floorboards in one of the semi-derelict rooms. There was a fragment of an old fireplace with a Tudor rose painted in red and green. A mysterious smashed miniature, its subject unrecognizable: 'It looked as if someone had ground their heel into it after a furious row; it was obviously quite deliberately smashed.' And a charming little lady's fob watch, made in green enamel and studded with pearls, diamonds and rubies. 'No one knows whose it was, but it goes very well to this day.' (Outdoor treasure hunting was less fruitful. Eric Evans is said to have dug trenches in the courtyard in search of a legendary hoard of buried plate. He discovered none. An enigmatic explanation has been offered: the treasure had already been found.)

We are indebted to Barbara Evans for a plausible explanation for at least one case of those mysterious floating lights that haunt the history of Aberglasney – we encountered them in Chapter Two, in the story of the maids. 'I knew the theory was that if you saw these candles burning, someone was going to die.' In this case they came after the death of her husband, not as a ghostly forewarning. She was coming into the hall when she saw a series of disembodied candle flames moving towards her. 'One night the generator was not working. I had lit a pair of candelabras with three candles. As I came down the stairs I saw the lights coming towards me. There were huge windows on either side of the front door. It was the reflection of the lights but not the candlesticks. Silver does not reflect.' This, she felt, could be how the whole myth had started. Mrs Evans had her feet firmly on the ground. She loved Aberglasney, was very happy there, and never for a moment felt spooked by anything in the least supernatural.

But (the storyteller remembers) our brief is to tell the story of the gardens! Things were in pretty good order, post-war. The 'Gloire de Dijon' rose was pruned and fertilized and performed well, grass was mown, the yew tunnel was clipped to shape,

The Mayhews

all with the help of the one gardener, Llywelyn Davies. The enclosures around the house fulfilled their proper function as places to be used and enjoyed. Children played on the lawns and grown-ups took drinks on the terrace. There was croquet and there were hunt balls and fancy-dress parties. In 1951 the Cloister Garden became a theatre as three hundred local children performed a splendid pageant celebrating the twenty-fifth anniversary of the Junior Red Cross, to a script by Barbara Evans, in which featured monks and nuns, the battle of Solferino, Florence Nightingale and Jean Henri Dunant, genius behind the Red Cross. 'The main actors could proclaim from the top of the Cloisters and the children did crowd scenes like the battle on the lawns.' Everyone loved the arches with their long stalactites, which intimated how long a time they must have taken to form.

The sudden death of Eric Evans in July 1950 following an operation at a London hospital shocked everyone. The trustees of the estate took the decision to sell up. There were different arguments, rational and perhaps irrational. At two thousand acres the

ABOVE *Heiress Mary Anne Pryse (left) married Lieutenant Charlie Mayhew (right) in December 1872 and they finally came to live at Aberglasney in 1902. Their chief claim to fame in the area was their addiction to the Temperance movement.*

BELOW *The Temperance Rally of 1905 drew hundreds to Aberglasney. The Mayhews used this photograph as their Christmas card that year. 'SUCCESS TO OUR BAND OF HOPE' reads the banner on the portico. The Mayhew party is in the centre of the crowd, the Colonel wearing a striped sash. Also among the sea of faces, it is said, is that of Evans the Bwlch, well known as the local tippler.*

estate was thought to be on the small side to form a viable economic proposition in the current climate. Michael Lyndon Skeggs, the sub-agent on the Cawdor estate who later married the widowed Barbara Evans, commented: 'The liability was considerable and the rents were very low. I could see no prospect of making a living there.' General I.P. Evans had other things on his mind. His wife, who should have inherited Aberglasney, had died at the age of twenty-four. His son, who did inherit, was dead at thirty. Perhaps there was some kind of curse on the place, which was known hardly ever to have passed simply from father to son. The General decidedly did not want his little grandsons to run the risk. 'He felt there was a bad feeling about the house. He was very anxious that it shouldn't be left to Christopher, that he shouldn't go and live there.' The General actively encouraged the family to sell up.

When the ownership of Aberglasney changes hands it is always attended by some kind of drama. Hardyesque overtones surrounded the sale of the Aberglasney lands in 1955. The powerful neighbouring landlord of Golden Grove had his eye on the estate in its entirety: his own extensive lands lapped Aberglasney's very garden walls, with Berllandywyll farm separating the estate from the Towy river. Attached to the Golden Grove demesne, the whole would make a fine and economically attractive holding. 'Lord Cawdor wanted the lot,' summed up Mrs Thomas of Broad Oak Farm.

Aberglasney's tenant farmers, on the other hand, were equally adamant in their desire to become owners of the land that some had worked for generations. Battle was locked, with solicitors Walters and Williams of Carmarthen handling the sale on behalf of the estate. The farmland was to be sold as a block, so six or seven or eight of the farmers joined together and met at Broad Oak Farm. Each time they put in a bid to Walters and Williams, Lord Cawdor would put in a higher one. There would be another meeting at Broad Oak Farm, another bid from the farmers, another answering bid from Lord Cawdor. In the end someone appealed to General Evans and George Pryse-Rice to intervene. The book was closed when they declared their intention 'not to be on top of the farmers'.[28]

At last the estate was broken up into separate farms. The purchaser of the mansion complex in which we are interested with its hamlet of outbuildings and cottages and a handful of fields – amounting to almost seventy acres – was David Charles. Here we have a hint of history repeating itself. As a prosperous lawyer with a practice in

ABOVE *'Marriage of VC's son' was the newspaper caption when Lieutenant Eric Evans of the Black Watch and Barbara Rogers WRNS were married in 1943. Other key figures in our story are Brigadier-General Evans himself (on the far left) and Dame Margaret Pryse-Rice, the groom's grandmother (third from left).*

Carmarthen, Aberglasney's new owner stood in the footsteps of the Robert Dyer who had bought Aberglasney in the early 1700s. Charles was not only a highly successful solicitor, but like Dyer acted as land agent for some of the big landowners in the area – he handled the affairs of the Edwinsford Estate, for example. He had been a captain in the Indian Army and was a keen horseman, an enthusiasm he shared with his wife Barbara. Although he did not yet live in the Big House, 'He was a colourful character, definitely the new lord of the manor, sitting in the front pew in church and reading the lesson.'[29]

Like Dyer, Charles seemed to have entered the ranks of the landed gentry. But whereas it took the best part of a century for later generations of Dyers to lose their grip on Aberglasney, David Charles achieved this in person inside a couple of decades. While around the new owner the world wove the dazzling web of myths and tales that we have to unravel to find the truth, the fabric of Aberglasney's gardens entered the most serious period of their decline.

David Charles bought the place for a song, installed his horses in the stables, his Welsh Blacks in the cowsheds and took up residence in one of the cottages. Occasionally parties and hunts balls were held in the hall of the mansion. Presumably Charles intended to set the building to rights in due course. Somehow this never happened. Why?

Here it is tempting for the storyteller to invoke 'spirits' as the cause of David Charles's deline – and not just the obvious ones. At this point we shall make one of our rare visits into the mansion itself – and the haunted mansion at that! – to make the acquaintance of the last people who actually lived within its walls. For a year or two after the departure of Mrs Eric Evans and her sons, a different family with the same surname had stayed on as resident caretakers, living in the parts of the house that were sound. Hugh and Elizabeth Evans remember being at that time 'very poor, but gloriously happy' at Aberglasney. When David Charles bought the property Hugh Evans did odd jobs in lieu of rent until they could find somewhere to live. In the Evanses we meet some valuable first-hand witnesses of unaccountable happenings in the house – sounds of footsteps, poltergeistly displacement of knicknacks and kitchen items, sightings by their baby daughter of a merry white-bearded old man invisible to everyone else. (Years later Frances asked her parents about the nice gentleman whom she remembered babysitting; they knew there was no such person.) The Evanses in their different ways seemed to get on rather well with whatever restless spirit might be behind these manifestations – unlike various village people, who flatly refused to visit the place, or who when they did come to the house found it decidedly unnerving. Hugh Evans himself talks of experiencing a 'warm glow' of benevolence from time to time both at Aberglasney and after they had left – it occurred once later when he handed in the Littlewoods coupon that won him a substantial dividend! It also happened to him in the mansion after he had had a confrontation with an overbearing David Charles. It was accompanied by a premonition that David Charles was heading for disaster. 'He started drinking heavily, and it was not long after that that his wife left him and he really started to go downhill.' Perhaps Charles got on the wrong side of Aberglasney's mysterious presence – the one with which the residents Hugh and Elizabeth Evans had evolved a happy *modus vivendi*. Perhaps David Charles had somehow offended the spirit of the place.

At this point we should perhaps cut to a scene in the White Hart, Llandeilo. It is a Saturday morning: almost any Saturday morning in the 1960s and early 1970s. A lively set of friends is drinking together. They are intelligent, educated, professional people; the conversation flows freely, as does the alcohol. Back from university, the army and a spell in London, local writer Lynn Hughes looked in one Saturday morning in the early 1970s. 'I got to know David at the White Hart. He was a *bon viveur* and the whole atmosphere at the White Hart was as if a Second World War party was still going on.' Many of Aberglasney's myths and legends were given an airing during these sessions, gaining further embellishments in the process; no doubt new ones were being engendered too.

The party carried on at Aberglasney: at least, the boozing and some of the *laissez-faire* attitudes. Drinking gradually got the better of David Charles. He was banned from driving years before the breathalyser came in. Neighbours and local people – even teetotallers! – were detailed to collect him from the Halfway Inn or to fetch him a bottle of whisky. These are memories, not myths. Soon after his wife left him, taking the children, his mistress moved in. She was David Charles's match at the bottle, and when she died surrounded by gin bottles, the coroner recorded a verdict of 'death by misadventure'.[29] Soon after this tragedy David Charles moved away and sold up.

Those are the sobering facts. Now the myths begin to crowd in: let's just consider those that have a bearing on the state of the gardens – rapidly transforming from well-tended pleasure grounds via quasi-farmyard to hopeless wilderness. Brambles and the creeping stolons of Japanese knotweed steadily invaded the untended grounds. A cameo of the Cloister Garden: David Charles, with none-too-steady gait, scything the long grass of the parapet walk and endangering the limbs of anyone watching. By the late 1970s you could still walk round the parapet, though it was impossible to cross the weed-choked gardens below. A neighbour says Charles kept pigs in the house. Someone else recalls pigs on the front lawn and corn in the front drawing room, adding that lead was stolen off the roof. In 1980 Aberglasney was 'now in decay, having been inhabited by goats during the last twenty years'.[30] All sounded topsy-turvy. Elfyn Rees – a reliable witness – knows nothings of pigs or goats in the house, but remembers two donkeys nibbling the bark of the fine cryptomeria in the Pool Garden (where the bottles-in-the-pond scenario that we have already encountered took place). The Upper Kitchen Garden was rotavated and planted up with potatoes for a couple of seasons when the market seemed favourable; the result was a permanent garden blight, since the potato-

planting obliterated the pattern of box-lined paths and invited in the opportunistic rank-weed population of disturbed ground. The yew trees and box bushes grew unkempt. More ivy seeded in the mortar of the walls and progressively smothered them with foliage, its roots prising apart the stones and stimulating that extra escalating dilapidation as it went. The mansion kept pace in the downward drift to dereliction.

At this stage in its history the wary average householder will look at Aberglasney and its garden structures with a shudder and walk sharply away. The historian will sigh over lost epochs of country-house life and social record and turn from the scene with a sad shake of the head. But a spectator of more romantic disposition will find charm and mystery in the decay. Aberglasney is good at exercising this kind of allure. In a way the next two purchasers fall into this last category. David Charles decided to sell up, aswe said. The time is March 1977. The scene is the White Hart in Llandeilo once again. Aberglasney Estate, nearly seventy acres, is offered for sale. What is under the hammer (in that breathless legal prose) consists of:

ABOVE Briefly after the war Aberglasney came alive again with parties, balls and gatherings in a different spirit from those of the Mayhews' worthy assemblies. In Festival of Britain year, Mrs Evans wrote a pageant enacting the story of the Red Cross, and the Cloister Garden played a starring role as the theatre.

All that Mansion House demesne cloisters outbuildings grounds woodlands and farm lands known as Aberglasney Broad Oak in the County of Dyfed together with the Keepers Cottage the two cottages near thereto and Pigeon House ALL which said property contains by admeasurement 69.848 acres or thereabouts. . .

Local people and strangers crowd into the function room to see what will become of the property. The buyer is neither local nor, indeed, strictly somebody. In due time Aberglasney is bought in its entirety by the disembodied entity known as John Owen Fine Arts and Investments Company Limited of Cardiff. The public thinks it's all over. But by no means. A muttered exchange takes place on the podium. The auctioneer turns to the crowd again. 'Ladies and Gentlemen – don't leave yet! We are offering the property split up into separate lots. In ten minutes. Just wait where you are.' The officials retire to an inner sanctum while the gasps of astonishment change into a crescendo of animated speculation.

When the auctioneer reappears and the lots have been sold, and sold on, Aberglasney has been subdivided into six, or seven, or maybe nine lots – separate dwellings like the individual lodges and cottages, some with pieces of land or a barn attached, or a potential building plot. It was a clever move. The modest extent of most of the new parcels made them a far more realistic proposition for ordinary people in search of a reasonably sized house with a little land, or a building to convert, or a modest investment of capital, or an adventure.

The last lot is the mansion and its gardens – not such an ordinary entity. But then, the forthcoming buyer and her partner are rather extraordinary people. They are the young widow Maggie Perry and the architect and builder Malcolm Miller.

The story behind their being in a position to buy Aberglasney is one of those larger-than-life human dramas whose telling lies outside our remit (it involves, for instance, an air disaster over Paris – far too far away and long ago to go into here). Let us meet them in action at Aberglasney a couple of years after the auction. They appear (literally) on our screen in *Pride of Place*, a BBC series on historic Welsh homes broadcast first in 1981 and again in 1986 – a kind of *Lost Houses of Wales* of Tom Lloyd brought to life. By this time they own not only the mansion, but also the pair of bailiff's houses, which they have converted. In the film Malcolm Miller is seen heroically scything away at waist-high undergrowth in front of the mansion like some pioneering frontiersman – Clint Eastwood would be spot-on cast in the part, though it looks like a battle he might lose. Maggie Perry approaches him through the leafage from the direction of the Yew Tunnel, striding like Diana the Huntress, wolfhounds at her heels. The Marquess of Anglesey's voice-over relishes a quote from John Dyer about neighbouring Dynevor's ruined castle: 'Much of Dyer's poem "Grongar Hill" has a disconcerting aptness today,' he says. 'So many of the lines can be applied to the present state of Aberglasney:

> 'Tis now the raven's bleak abode;
> 'Tis now th' apartment of the toad...
>
> Conceal'd in ruins, moss and weeds:
> While ever and anon there falls
> Huge heaps of hoary, moulder'd walls.
> Yet time has seen, that lifts the low,
> And level lays the lofty brow,
> Has seen this broken pile complete,
> Big with the vanity of state:
> But transient is the smile of Fate!

Confronted with decay that amounts to dereliction, one might well feel that Aberglasney should be left to its fate.' As he speaks the camera wanders back and forth over the crumbling fabric of the house, lingering over the sagging ceilings, blistering plaster, rotting timbers, colonizing weeds in the debris. The narrator alludes to the

RIGHT *A derelict mansion is open house to pilferers and vandals as well as to the elements. When the Restoration Trust took over, Aberglasney was at its lowest ebb, having lost even its portico. But its absence revealed the high quality of Robert Dyer's façade of c.1715 with its fashionable roundel above the doorcase, and provided other clues to the history of the building.*

youth, vigour and determination of the couple, but in the end is equivocal, enigmatic. 'Ultimately everybody has the right to let their house fall down around them.' The next scene cuts to some other lofty pile and shows it being demolished.

The serious decay that began with flooding in Mrs Mayhew's day and meant that parts of the house were unsafe during and after the war had since been exacerbated by human depradations, though when the couple bought the mansion it was still just about habitable. It was the garden rather than the house that attracted the pair to Aberglasney. 'It had something special about it. We could not resist it. A little secret garden it was then. A magical place.' One of Malcolm Miller's intentions – although they did not know quite what they would do with the house (restore a wing, perhaps) – was 'at the very least to put a lid on it to keep the rain out'. They did indeed repair the roof.

However, they were not living on site all the time, and by the time they returned from a trip away the lead had been stripped off again. Slowly, over a longer time than the Miller incumbency, the word had got around that there was 'architectural salvage' to be had, above or below board. In west Wales we often hear that an old chapel roof has been stripped of slates (always by Cowboys from the South); once word gets round that an old building is in that Interesting State of semi-repair, or is being done up (which means that the toing and froing of builders' lorries goes unquestioned) there's a free-for-all. Besides the overall picture of general decline two facts emerge that take our story towards its conclusion: the Millers fail to save Aberglasney, and they fail spectacularly because of legal action.

At Aberglasney the overiding fact is that for three decades or so, whatever the good intentions of the owners, the natural forces of rain, wind and gravity were exacerbated by human covetousness. It was open season for all. Slates (and lead) slid surreptitiously from roofs. Coping stones disappeared from the Cloister Garden parapet. Handsome ironwork gates slipped their moorings. Ornaments like weighty stone eagles took flight. Indoors, fireplaces and panelling dematerialized to grace new interiors. There was also sheer vandalism. Someone lit a fire in the fine hall. The historic stained-glass window painted with the heraldic device of John Walters Philipps was smashed. It comes almost as a relief to find that some objects and papers had intermittently been 'saved' over the years by rummaging visitors.[31]

Who was responsible? The rumours begin again. Malcolm Miller dates the start of the depradations to before his time: 'Half of Carmarthenshire had stuff from the mansion, everything from paintings to panelling. The going rate was a case of gin.' Malcolm Miller seems genuinely to have tried to save the place, Canute against the rising tide, a Sisyphean task. One house restorer said they tried to persuade Miller to let them have some much-coveted panelling but he would not let it go. The storyteller can name no names. But it is during Miller's incumbency that serious, systematic raiding took place. Floorboards from the house were laid lengthwise in pairs or threes over the soft mud around the house to make a firm track along which laden barrowloads of goodies could be wheeled more efficiently.

Eventually Miller himself became implicated. The climax came with the filching of Aberglasney's most prominent feature. Of all the unlikely, least portable of knicknacks, the weighty portico itself was in transit. It was tantamount to stealing the nose off a face, yet it happened. Miller returned to Aberglasney after an absence and found the said feature prepared by some unnamed third party for removal elsewhere, the pillars and capitals dismantled in sections on the ground – except, of course, for the pillar that had been hardest to detach. He removed the last bit (thus laying himself open to accusation of having tampered with a listed building) and transported the hundred-odd three-dimensional jigsaw pieces of stone for storage in the yard of another property of his, the old School House in Llandeilo, where he ran a wine bar and restaurant. The portico, in pieces, turned out to be a rather high-quality (and quite valuable) item. Many such a nineteenth-century piece proves under scrutiny (or demolition) to consist of a brick core rendered over to look like stone, but Aberglasney's famous columns are the real Monty – lathe-turned sections of limestone, bespoke to a classical model by some favoured early Victorian jobbing architect for his earnest patron. It is evidence that patron John Walters Philipps, spared little expense over his improvements at Aberglasney.

Later on, in 1993, the portico was offered for sale at Christie's, in the scenario which we previewed in Chapter One. The thwarting of that sale, the consequent court case, and the requirement of Dynevor Borough Council's listed buildings enforcement notice that the portico be retrieved and then 'restored to its former state' on a mansion that had been repaired and waterproofed gave a statutory, public dimension to the slow leaching away of Aberglasney's treasures. These high-profile events at last brought the fate of Aberglasney into the public eye – the place was now making headline news, although for a long time articles and features in local newspaper had been building into a scrapbook archive of background information and anecdote, while a little band of determined historic gardens enthusiasts had been machinating behind the scenes to try to save the place.

The court case made the rescue of Aberglasney a *cause célèbre*. It catalysed the formation of the Aberglasney Restoration Trust, although the very existence of the portico became a new subject of controversy, as parties debated whether the building was better without what some seemed to consider a 'Victorian monstrosity'. However laudable their intentions had once been to save Aberglasney, Malcolm Miller and Maggie Perry simply could not undertake the major work on the mansion that the enforcement notice required. After much negotiation they agreed to have the columns returned from Christie's and stored at a 'secret location' – and to sell Aberglasney to the Trust. The deal went through in the spring of 1995. The selling price was a mere £35,000 – but that was just the tip of an iceberg of funding that had to be sought. Miraculously (if that term can be consistent with extraordinary amounts of effort and feats of persuasion on the part of the Restoration Trust) the means gradually materialized. Gradually, the smothering vegetation and detritus of a generation were peeled back and an unsuspecting public became aware of the magnitude of Aberglasney's heritage.

Around the time of the sale of 1977, writer Lynn Hughes sounded a prophetic note in a *Western Mail* article.[32] Recalling John Dyer's appeal to 'Keep, ye gods, this humble seat / Forever pleasant, private, neat', he suggested that 'Some benefactor should buy it and donate it to the National Trust or the Arts Council to answer that prayer. It would make a perfect haven for painters and writers from cities to go into retreat. And nowhere in Wales is there such a setting for open-air concerts and drama.' Nowhere in Wales, nor indeed in Britain, is there such an extraordinary garden.

The Aberglasney Restoration Trust

'A BERGLASNEY IS OURS!' wrote William Wilkins on 1 April 1995, on behalf of the Aberglasney Restoration Trust, a charity specially set up to save the property. It was no April Fool: the purchase of the mansion complex was the culmination of years of watching, waiting, hoping and working. Once again the extraordinary switchback profile of Aberglasney's destiny was taking an upward turn. The offspring of a marriage between private enthusiasms and public backing, the newborn charity was endowed with a healthy hybrid vigour and independence. This was as well, for more work was beginning. One task was to convince the various Powers That Be to share the vision of the Trust's founders that here was something special that needed support and hard cash (this in the mid-1990s, when funding goalposts were being moved). Financial backing for restoring Aberglasney is partly private with generous contributions from an anonymous American benefactor, the Esmée Fairbairn Charitable Trust, the Garfield Weston Foundation and other foundations, trusts and individual donors, and is partly from public bodies including: Cadw: Welsh Historic Monuments; Carmarthenshire County Council; the European Regional Development Fund; the Heritage Lottery Fund; the Wales Tourist Board and the Welsh Development Agency.

Another task was to set about realizing that vision in the most complex of settings while at the same time attempting to discover what really was there. A tenet of the Trust's faith was that Aberglasney's extraordinary nature was to be matched in excellence by the people chosen to re-create it. 'Restoration' was in the name of the Trust, but it did not mean the mansion or its gardens were to be returned to some point in their history and held there in aspic. The idea was to bring them back to life, to a new, forward-looking reincarnation, respecting the past but using it to inspire the future. To this end top-class professionals and dedicated expertise came together to repair the fabric, design new plantings and create the extra features that human garden visitors require. They all rose to the occasion, inspired by what they found.

Aberglasney's physical transformation has swallowed up the creative energies of many, many creative people. Now she is ready to repay the debt. In opening to visitors she issues a challenge – to find inspiration here, and to celebrate in music, poetry, art, dance, stillness and sheer pleasure.

To this book about the gardens, Aberglasney mansion has stood as a backdrop: ghastly in dereliction, then gaping in repair. Under the scrutiny of archaeology it has shed the secrets of its evolution more slowly than have the gardens. That is another story.

RIGHT *A scale model showing an imaginative view of how the gardens might look when restored was a valuable tool in the Trust's early days of raising support and funds.*

BELOW *During the restoration visitors marvelled at the changes. Some of this group of Historic Houses enthusiasts (including speaker Tom Lloyd) had witnessed the stages of Aberglasney's decline.*

The Yew Tunnel in Winter

BY GILLIAN CLARKE

Listen to sap rise, unstoppable flood,
for each of its thousand years as the the tap-roots grew,
pumping through branches to the stirring bud
from deepest earth. In graveyards, they say, a yew

sends a root into the mouths of all the dead.
Here, sense all that power snowed in and still,
shut in the dream of winter and history
at the end of a muffled lane below Grongar Hill.

The garden's underwraps. The sorrow trees
let in, like moonlight, little webs of snow,
white footfalls through the arching clerestories
Grown from seed ten centuries ago

from the gut of a bird, the Age of Hywel done,
the poetry of gardens yet to come.

Map of Restored Garden

Key

1 Yew Tunnel
2 North Lawn
3 Gatehouse Court
4 Portico
5 Aberglasney House
6 Gardener's House

7 Gardener's Cottage
8 Parapet Walk
9 Cloister Garden
10 Bishop Rudd's Walk
11 Church View Wood
12 Aviary

13 Upper Walled Garden
14 Kitchen Garden
15 Pool Garden
16 Stream Garden
17 Pigeon House Wood

METRES

0 10 20 30 40 50 60 70 80 90 100

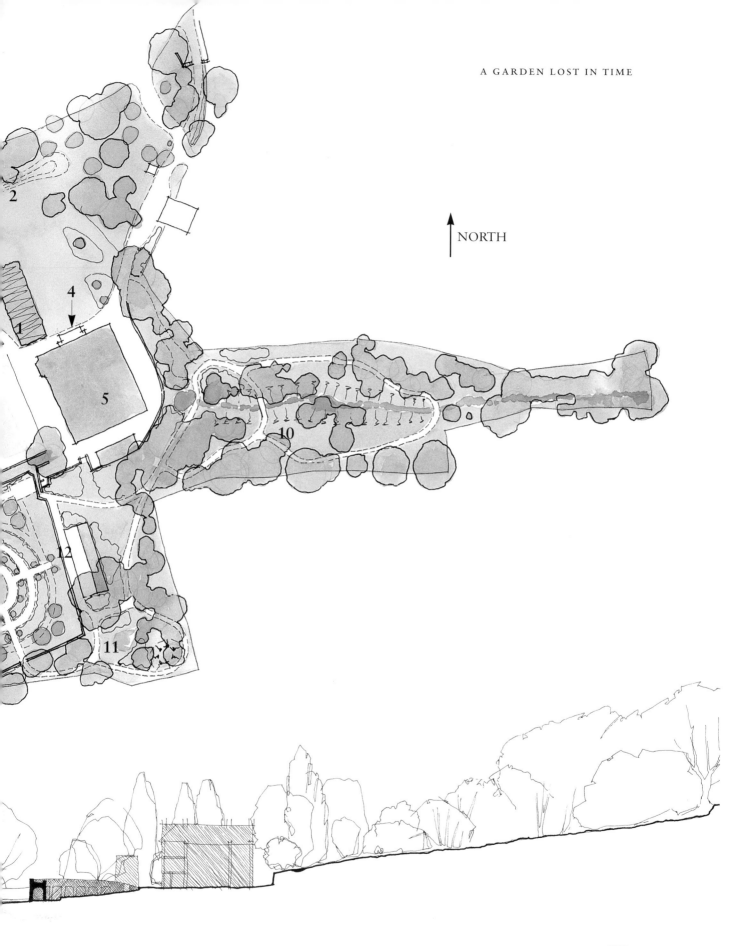

NORTH

Family Trees

TABLE I: Antecedents of the Thomas family who owned Aberglasney (Plas Llangathen) in the Sixteenth Century

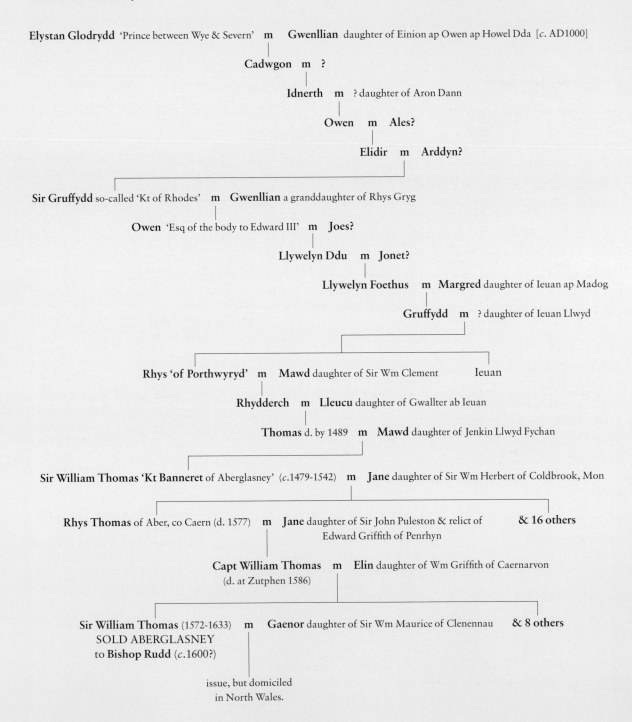

Elystan Glodrydd 'Prince between Wye & Severn' m Gwenllian daughter of Einion ap Owen ap Howel Dda [*c.* AD1000]

Cadwgon m ?

Idnerth m ? daughter of Aron Dann

Owen m Ales?

Elidir m Arddyn?

Sir Gruffydd so-called 'Kt of Rhodes' m Gwenllian a granddaughter of Rhys Gryg

Owen 'Esq of the body to Edward III' m Joes?

Llywelyn Ddu m Jonet?

Llywelyn Foethus m Margred daughter of Ieuan ap Madog

Gruffydd m ? daughter of Ieuan Llwyd

Rhys 'of Porthwyryd' m Mawd daughter of Sir Wm Clement   Ieuan

Rhydderch m Lleucu daughter of Gwallter ab Ieuan

Thomas d. by 1489 m Mawd daughter of Jenkin Llwyd Fychan

Sir William Thomas 'Kt Banneret of Aberglasney' (*c.*1479-1542) m Jane daughter of Sir Wm Herbert of Coldbrook, Mon

Rhys Thomas of Aber, co Caern (d. 1577) m Jane daughter of Sir John Puleston & relict of   & 16 others
Edward Griffith of Penrhyn

Capt William Thomas m Elin daughter of Wm Griffith of Caernarvon
(d. at Zutphen 1586)

Sir William Thomas (1572-1633) m Gaenor daughter of Sir Wm Maurice of Clenennau   & 8 others
SOLD ABERGLASNEY
to Bishop Rudd (*c.*1600?)

issue, but domiciled
in North Wales.

TABLE II: The Rudds of Carmarthenshire: the Seventeenth Century

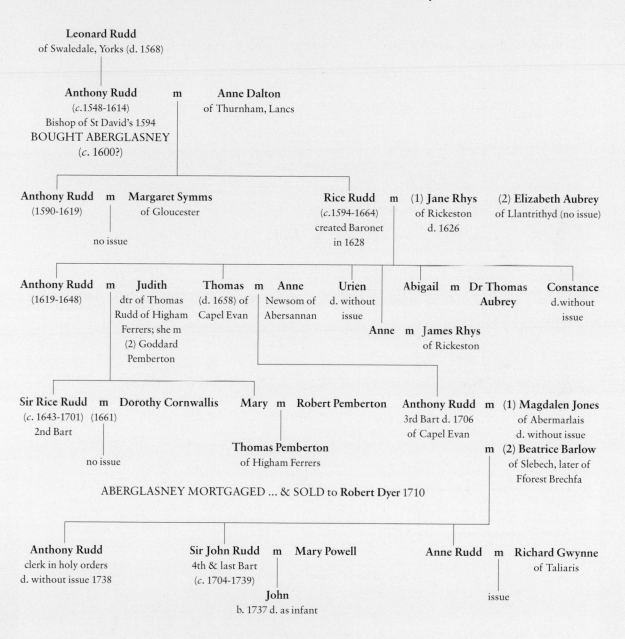

Leonard Rudd
of Swaledale, Yorks (d. 1568)

Anthony Rudd m **Anne Dalton**
(*c*.1548-1614) of Thurnham, Lancs
Bishop of St David's 1594
BOUGHT ABERGLASNEY
(*c*. 1600?)

Anthony Rudd m **Margaret Symms** **Rice Rudd** m (1) **Jane Rhys** (2) **Elizabeth Aubrey**
(1590-1619) of Gloucester (*c*.1594-1664) of Rickeston of Llantrithyd (no issue)
created Baronet d. 1626
no issue in 1628

Anthony Rudd m **Judith** **Thomas** m **Anne** **Urien** **Abigail** m **Dr Thomas** **Constance**
(1619-1648) dtr of Thomas (d. 1658) of Newsom of d. without **Aubrey** d.without
Rudd of Higham Capel Evan Abersannan issue issue
Ferrers; she m
(2) Goddard **Anne** m **James Rhys**
Pemberton of Rickeston

Sir Rice Rudd m **Dorothy Cornwallis** **Mary** m **Robert Pemberton** **Anthony Rudd** m (1) **Magdalen Jones**
(*c*. 1643-1701) (1661) 3rd Bart d. 1706 of Abermarlais
2nd Bart of Capel Evan d. without issue
no issue **Thomas Pemberton** m (2) **Beatrice Barlow**
of Higham Ferrers of Slebech, later of
Fforest Brechfa

ABERGLASNEY MORTGAGED ... & SOLD to **Robert Dyer** 1710

Anthony Rudd **Sir John Rudd** m **Mary Powell** **Anne Rudd** m **Richard Gwynne**
clerk in holy orders 4th & last Bart of Taliaris
d. without issue 1738 (*c*. 1704-1739)
John issue
b. 1737 d. as infant

TABLE III: The Dyers of Aberglasney: the Eighteenth Century

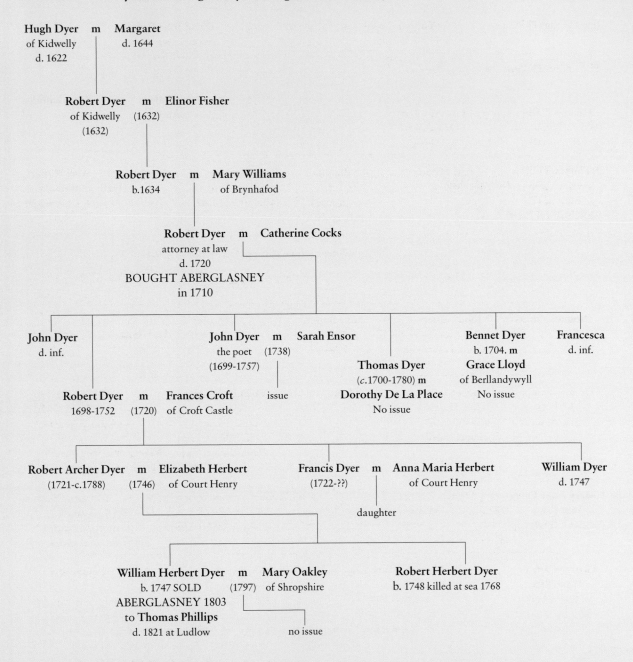

Hugh Dyer   **m**   **Margaret**
of Kidwelly   d. 1644
d. 1622

Robert Dyer   **m**   **Elinor Fisher**
of Kidwelly   (1632)
(1632)

Robert Dyer   **m**   **Mary Williams**
b.1634   of Brynhafod

Robert Dyer   **m**   **Catherine Cocks**
attorney at law
d. 1720
BOUGHT ABERGLASNEY
in 1710

John Dyer   **John Dyer**   **m**   **Sarah Ensor**   **Bennet Dyer**   **Francesca**
d. inf.   the poet   (1738)   b. 1704. m   d. inf.
       (1699-1757)   **Thomas Dyer**   **Grace Lloyd**
                         (*c*.1700-1780) m   of Berllandywyll

Robert Dyer   **m**   **Frances Croft**   issue   **Dorothy De La Place**   No issue
1698-1752   (1720)   of Croft Castle   No issue

Robert Archer Dyer   **m**   **Elizabeth Herbert**   **Francis Dyer**   **m**   **Anna Maria Herbert**   **William Dyer**
(1721-c.1788)   (1746)   of Court Henry   (1722-??)   of Court Henry   d. 1747

daughter

William Herbert Dyer   **m**   **Mary Oakley**   **Robert Herbert Dyer**
b. 1747 SOLD   (1797)   of Shropshire   b. 1748 killed at sea 1768
ABERGLASNEY 1803
to **Thomas Phillips**
d. 1821 at Ludlow   no issue

TABLE IV: Aberglasney's Owners (* asterisked) in the Nineteenth and Twentieth Centuries

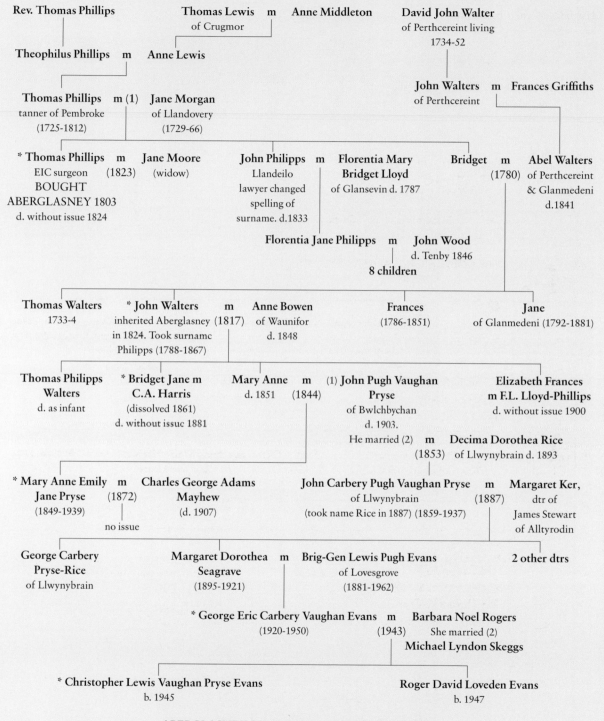

Rev. Thomas Phillips

Thomas Lewis m Anne Middleton
of Crugmor

David John Walter
of Perthcereint living
1734-52

Theophilus Phillips m Anne Lewis

John Walters m Frances Griffiths
of Perthcereint

Thomas Phillips m (1) Jane Morgan
tanner of Pembroke   of Llandovery
(1725-1812)   (1729-66)

* Thomas Phillips m Jane Moore
EIC surgeon (1823) (widow)
BOUGHT
ABERGLASNEY 1803
d. without issue 1824

John Philipps m Florentia Mary
Llandeilo   Bridget Lloyd
lawyer changed of Glansevin d. 1787
spelling of
surname. d.1833

Bridget m Abel Walters
(1780) of Perthcereint
& Glanmedeni
d.1841

Florentia Jane Philipps m John Wood
d. Tenby 1846
8 children

Thomas Walters
1733-4

* John Walters m Anne Bowen
inherited Aberglasney (1817) of Waunifor
in 1824. Took surname d. 1848
Philipps (1788-1867)

Frances
(1786-1851)

Jane
of Glanmedeni (1792-1881)

Thomas Philipps
Walters
d. as infant

* Bridget Jane m
C.A. Harris
(dissolved 1861)
d. without issue 1881

Mary Anne m
d. 1851 (1844)

(1) John Pugh Vaughan
Pryse
of Bwlchbychan
d. 1903.
He married (2) m Decima Dorothea Rice
(1853) of Llwynybrain d. 1893

Elizabeth Frances
m F.L. Lloyd-Phillips
d. without issue 1900

* Mary Anne Emily m Charles George Adams
Jane Pryse (1872) Mayhew
(1849-1939)   (d. 1907)
no issue

John Carbery Pugh Vaughan Pryse m Margaret Ker,
of Llwynybrain   (1887) dtr of
(took name Rice in 1887) (1859-1937) James Stewart
of Alltyrodin

George Carbery
Pryse-Rice
of Llwynybrain

Margaret Dorothea m Brig-Gen Lewis Pugh Evans
Seagrave   of Lovesgrove
(1895-1921)   (1881-1962)

2 other dtrs

* George Eric Carbery Vaughan Evans m Barbara Noel Rogers
(1920-1950)   (1943) She married (2)
Michael Lyndon Skeggs

* Christopher Lewis Vaughan Pryse Evans
b. 1945

Roger David Loveden Evans
b. 1947

ABERGLASNEY SOLD 1956 to * David Morse Charles

ABERGLASNEY SOLD 1977 to * Margaret Ann Perry (via John Owen Fine Art & Investment Co)

ABERGLASNEY SOLD 1995 to * Aberglasney Restoration Trust

Bibliography & endnotes

Two indispensable sources of information about Aberglasney are works by the late Major Francis Jones, Wales Herald Extraordinary. His article 'Aberglasney and its Families' in *National Library of Wales Journal* vol. XXI (1979) – abbreviated hereafter as 'FJ (1979)' – gives an excellent précis of Aberglasney's owners. *Historic Carmarthenshire Homes and their Families* (1997) – abbreviated as 'FJ (1997)' – complements this account with valuable descriptions of where they and their neighbours lived. Other abbreviations used here:

ART: Aberglasney Restoration Trust

CAS: Carmarthenshire Archives Service

NLW: National Library of Wales

TCAS: *Transactions of the Carmarthenshire Antiquarian Society and Field Club*

WHGT: Welsh Historic Gardens Trust

Further reading

Lynn Hughes, *A Carmarthenshire Anthology* (1984)

Belinda Humfrey, *John Dyer* (1980)

J.E. Lloyd, *A History of Carmarthenshire,* Vols I and II (1935)

Thomas Lloyd, *Lost Houses of Wales* (1989)

M.A. Rudd, *Records of the Rudd Family* (1920)

J. Towyn-Jones, *The Ghosts of Aberglasney: the Origins of a Tradition* (1999)

Elizabeth Whittle, *The Historic Gardens of Wales* (1992)

Endnotes

Chapter One

1. Translation by Dafydd Johnston.

2. I.e. the commote of Catheiniog, the subdivision of an administrative district equivalent to an English hundred.

3. Dr Enid Pierce-Roberts, *Tai Uchelwyr y Beirdd 1350–1650* (1986) p. 23. The Welsh 'ystrydoedd' translates as 'streets'.

4. Cadw: Welsh Historic Monuments, Ref No: 20/22/130.

5. Isaac Ware, *Complete Body of Architecture* (1756).

6. 'Yfed gwin ynghanol gwrych/Mewn neuadd wych gelynen.' In Ffransis G. Payne, 'Yr Hen Ardd Gymreig', Lleufer (1955) pp. 55–66, trans. John Trefor.

7. Robert Turner, *Botanologia: The Brittish Physician* (1664).

8. Sir Thomas Browne, *Hydriotaphia* (1658).

9. *Annales Cambriae* (translation) p. 93, quoted in D. Llwyd

Isaac, 'The Battle of Coed Llathen', *Archaeologica Cambrensis* (1872) 4th Series no IX p. 53.

10. Dr Powel's *History of Wales*, edit. 1697 quoted in D. Llwyd Isaac, op. cit.

11. J.E. Lloyd, *A History of Carmarthenshire* (1935) I p. 189.

12. P.C. Bartrum notes (p. 406) that 'Gruffudd [sic] is never called "Sir" until the time of Lewys Dwnn who calls him Knight of Rhodes (i. 310, ii. 152)'. Pedigrees were often embroidered with such detail by later genealogists. FJ (1979) calls Gruffydd the first of the descendants of the eleventh-century chieftain Elystan Glodrydd to have associations with Carmarthenshire, but some genealogies put the name of Llangathen some five generations earlier. T.E. Griffiths in *Pedigrees of Carnarvonshire and Anglesey* (1914) p. 202, described Elystan Glodrydd himself as 'Prince between the Wye and Severn, of Llangathen and Porthwyryd, Carmarthen'.

13. R.R. Davies, *The Revolt of Owain Glyndwr* (1995) p. 56.

14. J.E. Lloyd, op. cit.

15. FJ (1979) p. 4.

16. Llangathen parishioners to whom odes were addressed included Llywelyn ap Gwilym ap Rhys of Brynhafod, his brother Henry ap Gwilym of Court Henry, Gwilym ap Thomas Fychan of Cefn Melgoed (later Cadfan) and the owners of Lanlash and Glandiwlas. See FJ (1997).

17. Dafydd Johnston, pers. comm.

18. Since Lewis Glyn Cothi died in 1489 Thomas ap Rhydderch must have predeceased him.

19. R.R. Davies, op.cit.

20. Ralph A. Griffiths, *The Principality of Wales in the Later Middle Ages* (1972) vol I, pp. 205–6.

21. A poem by Dafydd ap Hywel ab Ieuan Fechan survives, praising Sir William's character and military prowess.

22. He was the High Sheriff of Anglesey in 1563 and of Carnarvonshire in 1574; see T.E. Griffiths, op. cit.

23. RCAHMW *Inventory of the Ancient Monuments in Carnarvonshire* (1956) vol I, East p. 3.

24. FJ (1979) p. 5.

25. His wife was Elen Griffith, descended from both the powerful Sir William Griffith, Chamberlain of Gwynedd, and the eminent Wynns of Gwydir. See T.E. Griffiths, op.cit.

Chapter Two

1. Paula Henderson points out that the word 'cloister' did not necessarily have monastic connotations, but was used to describe a loggia, arcade or colonnade. ART (1995).

2. M.A. Rudd (1920): Francis Jones calls the father Robert.

3. Fuller, *Church History of Britain* (1655), p. 69.

4. Aikin, *Memoirs of the Court of Queen Elizabeth*.

5. The new coat of arms is described as '*azure* a chevron ermine between three bells *argent*': see FJ (1979) p. 8.

6. Historical Mss Commission, *Calendar of the manuscripts of the most Honourable Marquess of Salisbury at Hatfield House*, vol XII, p. 77; vol XII p. 611.

7. M.A. Rudd (1920) p. 62.

8. Edward Yardley, *Menevia Sacra* (1927) p. 103 (ed. Francis Green).

9. Variant spellings of Rhys/Rice/Rees and so on are not uncommon names in Wales. In Chapter One we met Rhydderch ap Rhys in Lewis Glyn Cothi's poem, as well as his descendant Rhys Thomas – both men connected with Llangathen.

10. The Rices of Dynevor and the family of Sir Rice's first wife – the Rhyses of Rickeston in Brawdy, Pembs – both claimed descent from Urien.

11. E.g. free warren in capital messages including Aberglasney and Abersannan and in lordships, among them 'Cethiniog', Dryslwyn and Alltygaer. See FJ (1979) p. 8.

12. All hearth ratings from FJ (1997) passim.

13. Robert Burton (1577–1640), *History of the Principality of Wales* (second ed. 1730). John Davis was vicar of Llanfihangel Genau'r Glyn, near Aberystwyth, in Cards. in the 1650s. See also T. Gwynn Jones, *Welsh Folklore and Folk Customs* (1930).

14. Lynn Hughes quoted in Peter Underwood, *Ghosts of Wales* (1978) p. 109.

15. NLWMS 23296B, p. 34.

16. Idris Davies, undated article.

17. Ralph Mayer, *The Artist's Handbook*, pp. 50, 89–90.

18. Rory Young letter to author, 14 September 1998.

19. 'Now in an advanced state of decay [but] once one of the finest houses in the county': RCAHMW (1981) p. 178. Llantrithyd was built *c.* 1500–50 by a branch of the Bassets of Old Beaupre; its gardens were probably laid out subsequently by Anthony Mansel, who married into the family. See Elizabeth Whittle, *The Historic Gardens of Wales* (1992) p. 16.

20. Ibid.

21. Stephen Briggs, 'The Fabric of Parklands and Gardens in the Tywi Valley and beyond', *The Carmarthenshire Antiquary* vol xxxiii (1997) pp. 90–91.

22. Stephen Briggs, 'Interference and evidence in Welsh gardens and landscapes since c 1450', *There by Design: Field Archaeology in Parks and Gardens* (ed. Paul Pattison), RCHME (1998) p. 73.

23. See M.A. Rudd (1920) p. 74. Anne Rudd married her cousin german James ap Rice of Rickeston. Abigail married into her stepmother's family: her husband was Dr Thomas Aubrey, brother of Sir John Aubrey, Bart.

24. From the farmstead of Abersannan, which has connections with the Dyer family. A properties sold by Sir William Thomas to Bishop Rudd in 1605. See FJ (1997) p. 4; shortly afterwards Thomas Newsham or Newsom, a Carmarthen businessman, settled there; his daughter Ann married Thomas Rudd.

25. The Cornwallises had other Carmarthenshire links: in 1665 Dorothy's brother Sir Francis married the heiress of the fine Abermarlais estate. See FJ (1997) p. 4.

26. After the death of Anthony Rudd, Judith married Goddard Pemberton, probably of the same family as the husband of her daughter (Sir Rice's sister) Mary.

27. FJ (1979) p. 9.

28. Sir Anthony lived at Capel Evan, which he leased from the second baronet; later, through his wife Beatrice, heiress of Sir John Lloyd of Brechfa, he was mainly based at Fforest. He was buried in Carmarthen, not at Llangathen.

29. The chapel at Dryslwyn Castle, in this parish, was served by nuns of St Mary's Priory, Chester. See J.E. Lloyd, op. cit., vol I, p. 299; Rhys Dafis Williams, 'Llangathen and Aberglasney' in *Carmarthen Antiquary* III (3 & 4) (1961) p. 205.

30. Allen Samuels and John Dixon Hunt, 'Aberglasney: "an enigmatic cloister range"', *Journal of Garden History* (1991), vol 11, no 3, pp. 131–9.

31. Comparison made by Samuels and Dixon Hunt, op. cit.

32. Roy Strong, *The Renaissance Garden in England* (1984) pp. 144–5.

Chapter Three

1. Christopher K. Currie, 'Fishponds as Garden Features, c. 1550–1750', *Garden History* 18, pp. 22–40.

2. Col. Mayhew, 'Aberglasney', *TCAS* (1905) vol I p. 156.

3. Currie, op. cit.

4. Thomas Pennant, *Tour in Wales* (1784), quoted by William Condry, *The Natural History of Wales*, 2nd ed.(1990) pp. 180–81.

5. C. Anne Wilson, *Food and Drink in Britain* (1991 ed.) pp. 117, 121.

6. Condry, op. cit.

7. Ralph M. Williams, *Poet, Painter and Parson: the Life of John Dyer* (1956) p. 23.

8. J.P. Hylton Dyer Longstaffe, *Montgomeryshire Collections* XI (1878) p. 396.

9. Diary of Erasmus Philipps: NLW MS 23273 A.

10. One local tradition suggests this was Whitlera near Abersannan, where the family ran a mill and dyed cloth, but this seems an elaboration of a pun on the surname. See R. M. Williams, op. cit., p. 21.

11. Ralph M. Williams, 'Robert Dyer the Elder of Aberglasney, Gent.', in *TCAS* vol II part iii (1951) pp. 82–3.

12. Ibid.

13. Belinda Humfrey, *John Dyer* (1980) pp. 7–8. 'Kaglassran' is probably the mansion of Caeglas, just south of Llandeilo.

14. FJ (1979) p. 11.

15. Lewis Glyn Cothi wrote laudatory odes to one of its fifteenth-century owners; a mansion of five hearths in 1670, it was described in the 1830s as 'a very nice, dry, healthy gentleman-like place'. See FJ (1997) p. 16.

16. NLW MS 23294 D.

17. Ralph M. Williams (1956) p. 73.

18. Francis Jones, 'Portraits and Pictures in Old Carmarthenshire Houses', *The Carmarthenshire Historian* (1968) vol V pp. 45–6.

19. FJ (1979) p. 13.

20. Extracts reprinted from The Commonplace book as appendix to FJ (1979).

21. Quoted in Francis Jones (1968).

22. Revd Francis Coventry in the magazine *The World*, published between 1753–56 (no 15, 12 April 1753).

23. Jane Loudon, *The Lady's Country Companion* (1845) p. 323.

24. Diary of Mary Anne Pryse in CAS.

25. NLW MS 23294 D p. 75.

26. 'How can a man write poetically of serges and druggets?' he wrote about *The Fleece*. Quoted in Humfrey, op. cit. p. 77.

Chapter Four

1. From John Dyer's 1716 version of 'Grongar Hill'.

2. C. & A.M. Hall, *The Book of the Wye, South Wales and the Coast* (1861) p. 372.

3. Both were published in Richard Savage's *Miscellanies* (1726). See Humfrey, op. cit. p. 108.

4. Ibid. p. 105, quoting Gilpin's *Observations of the River Wye and sundry parts of South Wales* (1770).

5. Ralph M. Williams (1951) p. 88.

6. NLW MS 23297 B.

7. Humfrey op. cit. p. 13 quoting Richardson's 'Essay on the Theory of Painting' (1715).

8. Letter to Lady Beaumont in 1811 about *The Fleece*, quoted in Humfrey, op. cit. p. 2.

9. Willard Connely, *Sir Richard Steele*, p. 414.

10. The Steeles lived at Ty Gwyn, Llangunnor, incidentally a property owned by Bishop Rudd in 1609–10.

11. Willard Connely, op. cit. p. 413. The fellow-poet Robert is thought to be a cousin who wrote 'An Epistle to the Hon. Elizabeth Trevor', Sir Richard's daughter in 1732. Letter from Tom Lloyd 21 Oct 1998.

12. Letter from Rome *c.* 1724. Quoted in Humfrey, op. cit. p. 31.

13. ART (1995) p. 5.

14. Connely, op. cit. p. 414.

15. Benjamin Heath Malkin, *The Scenery, Antiquities and Bibliography of South Wales* (1804/7).

16. Connely, op. cit. p. 418.

17. Ralph M. Williams (1956) p. 36.

18. Humfrey, op. cit. pp. 70–71.

19. NLW MS 23294 D.

20. R. Gwynn Ellis, *Aliens in the British Flora* (1993).

21. R.J. Thomas, *Enwau Afonydd a Nentydd Cymru* (1938).

22. CAS Aberglasney 21/544 'Disbursements 1803–5'.

23. C. & M.A. Hall, op. cit.

24. Alan Stepney-Gulston, 'Aberglasney' in *TCAS* (1905) vol I, p. 156.

25. M.A . Rudd, op. cit. p. 62.

Chapter Five

1. Thomas Nicholas, *Annals and Antiquities of the Counties and County Families of Wales* (1872) records Mrs Harries as 'in residence'. Bridget Jane, who succeeded to the estate on her father's death in 1865 had married C.A. Harries of Llanunwas, Pembs. in 1853 but they separated in 1861 (the separation settlement is a formidable document: CAS Aberglasney 6/13).

2. ART archives: 'preliminary draft' 20 March 1995.

3. Unless otherwise indicated, the following account is based on FJ (1979).

4. The family lived at Penhill in Llangathen, where in the late 1600s their grandfather Theophilus Phillips made a well-connected marriage to Anne Lewes of Crugmor near Cardigan. (Her mother was a Middleton of Middleton Hall, and the descendants treasured the memory of her grandfather, a Ranger of Hyde Park under Charles II.)

5. Quoted in FJ (1997) p. 132.

6. Tom Lloyd, pers. comm.

7. CAS, Aberglasney Schedule: diary of Mary Anne Pryse. Entries for 3 Feb 1868 and 8 April 1869.

8. Susan Campbell, *Charleston Kedding* (1996) p. 87.

9. CAS, Aberglasney 14/363.

10. Prys Morgan, notes in ART archives.

11. Francis Jones, 'Walters of Perthcereint', *Ceredigion: Journal of the Cardiganshire Antiquarian Society* vol VI (1968–71) pp. 168–97.

12. The sisters were also avid collectors of autographs and franks. Later the seals and signatures of ministers were exchanged in earnest as the ageing ladies were caught up in brushes with the Rebecca rioters in south-west Cardiganshire where they lived at Glan Medeni.

13. ART archives: John Savidge, report of 15 May 1998.

Chapter Six

1. Idris Davies, notes in ART archives.

2. Idris Davies, Elfyn Rees, pers. comm.

3. Francis Jones (ed.) 'Journal of a Young Lady of Fashion' *The*

Carmarthenshire Historian 1974 ix p. 47.

4. Elizabeth Frances, youngest of the Walters Philipps sisters, married Frederick Lewis Lloyd-Phillips of Pentypark in 1851. Hafod Neddyn once belonged to a descendant of Llywelyn Foethus. It was purchased by John Walters Philipps around the time of his daughter's marriage and may have been intended to be their residence.

5. Cambrian Archaeological Association. *Report of Proceedings* (1892).

6. Letter in possession of C.L.V.P. Evans.

7. CAS, Aberglasney Box 33. The address is Ystradwrallt. The writer might have been Emma Ellen Philipps of that place, later Mrs A.W. J. Stokes (FJ (1997) p. 204.

8. CAS, Aberglasney Box 33: letters from Hardisty, Rhodes & Hardisty.

9. Mayhew served as Adjutant to the 2nd V.B. Derbyshire Volunteers in 1881–6, and Brigade Major to the North Midland Volunteers from 1888 to his retirement in 1904. See obituary notice in *Carmarthen Journal* 1 November 1907.

10. Idris Davies article, *Towy Valley Guardian* (9 March 1995).

11. Ibid. 'The entire cost of the Temperance Hall was borne by Mrs Mayhew', *Carmarthen Journal* (18 May 1906).

12. David Thomas Rees, pers. comm.

13. Valuation for probate of 3 April 1940 in possession of C.L.V.P. Evans.

14. Lynn Hughes, pers. comm. See also 'Mayhew's Mayhem' and 'The Curse of Grongar Hill', reprinted in Lynn Hughes's excellent *Carmarthenshire Anthology* (1984).

15. Barbara Lyndon Skeggs, interview.

16. H.J. Lloyd-Jones, 'Aberglasney's Catalogue of Weal', *The Carmarthenshire Historian* vol XV (1978) pp. 87–8. A note of the proceeds is in Eric Evans, 'Abstract': MS in possession of C.L.V.P. Evans.

17. CAS, Aberglasney Box 33: draft of letter dated 27 October 1909 (possibly by J.C.V. Pryse-Rice of Llwynybrain?) to unknown addressee.

18. Undated letter from Joseph Hallett in possession of C.L.V.P. Evans. Letter of 1934 CAS, Aberglasney Box 33.

19. Llwynybrain is eight miles eastwards along the A40. The Pryse-Rices' eldest daughter was heiress to Aberglasney and for

some years the fortunes of the two houses had become interwoven. Llwynybrain belonged briefly to Sir Rice Rudd of Aberglasney from 1625 to 1649, when he sold it to Samuel Hughes of Penhill, Llangathen. It is still in the possession of his descendants, having passed through several surviving female heirs. One was Decima Dorothea Rice, stepmother of Mrs Mayhew and mother-in-law to Dame Margaret.

20. Barbara Lyndon Skeggs, interview.

21. Letter WWJ to MPR 18/9/39 in possession of C.L.V.P. Evans.

22. The connection might have come through Mrs Mayhew's aunt Lloyd-Phillips, who had left some money 'to be held on trusts for the lives of the Collins family', but the origins of the association remain a mystery. See letters from W. Wilding Jones to Dame Margaret 22/2/1940 and 23/9/1940.

23. The descent can be traced in the family trees (see pp. 180–4).

24. D.T. Rees, interview 26 August 1988.

25. Letter to Capt G.C. Pryse-Rice (5 Oct 1940) in possession of C.L.V.P. Evans.

26. Michael Wisehall, pers. comm.

27. Idris Davies, undated article '7 maids die'.

28. Mrs Thomas, interview.

29. Stand-first in Lynn Hughes article, 'The Curse of Grongar Hill', *Western Mail Weekend Magazine* (1977).

30. Humfrey, op. cit.

31. Neil Hamilton, 'The next Heligan', *Weekend Telegraph* (26 December 1998).

32. Lynn Hughes, op. cit.

ACKNOWLEDGEMENTS

The first round of thanks is due to the Trustees and Staff of the Aberglasney Restoration Trust, who put archive material at my disposal, kept me up to date with new discoveries and were unfailingly patient when faced with persistent questioning. Particularly fond thanks to Frank Cabot, Elwyn Couser, Ayshea Cunniffe-Thomas, Peter Gosling, Graham Rankin, Elfyn Rees, Barbara Thomas, Eleri Thorpe, Liz Verbinnen, and above all to William Wilkins, as well as to now-departed Michael Thurlow and Gillian Windsor Morgan.

Thanks too to others directly involved in various ways with the mud and the mystery attending Aberglasney's restoration, especially Kevin Blockley, Sabine Eiche, Phil Evans, Stuart Gray, Craig Hamilton, Paula Henderson, Penelope Hobhouse, Mike Ibbotson, Tom Lloyd, Hal Moggridge, Andrew Sclater, John Trefor, Stephen Twamley and Dick Vigers.

Farther afield thanks are due for help of all kinds to: Stephen Briggs, Idris Davies, Lynn Davies, Peter Davis, Christopher Evans, Hugh and Elizabeth Evans, Neil Hamilton, Edward Harris, Lynn Hughes, Nigel Hughes, Roger Hughes, Belinda Humfrey, Dafydd Johnston, Barbara and Michael Lyndon Skeggs, Christine McCann, Margaret Messent, Malcolm Miller and Margaret Perry, Donald Moore, Prys Morgan, Joy Neal, Mick Nixon, Michael Norman, Jean O'Neill, John Phibbs, David Thomas Rees, Rosemary Rooney, John Savidge, Michael Powell Siddons, Harriet Thomas, Andrew Threipland, J. Towyn-Jones, Diana Uhlman, Betty Watson, Michael Wisehall, Rory Young, West Wales Dowsers Society and staff at Carmarthen Reference Library, Carmarthenshire Archives Service and the National Library of Wales.

On the book front I congratulate Kathy de Witt for her brilliant photographs, Nigel Soper on his elegant design, acknowledge Elizabeth Loving's helpful picture research, Tim Whiting's stalwart service at Weidenfeld HQ, but above all to thank Michael Dover for his confidence and support (and occasional intransigence) and Marilyn Inglis, editor extraordinaire, for encouragingly and intrepidly working to deadline. On the home front huge thanks to my husband Maurice Rotheroe, the 'but for whom' figure whose interviewing, reading and listening skills have been matched only by his much-needed support and love.

Despite these legions of help, the author must take responsibility as her own for the opinions and errors in the book (though not the choice of some spellings!), and hope that any readers who have corrections or further information will kindly pass them on via the Publishers or the Aberglasney Restoration Trust.

Index

DEDICATION

For the late Fred David, historian; for Beryl David, gardener; for Maurice Rotheroe, my mate; and for everyone who has ever haunted, or been haunted by, Aberglasney.

Text copyright © Penny David

Design and layout copyright
© Weidenfeld & Nicolson 1999

First published in 1999 by Weidenfeld & Nicolson

A CIP catalogue record for this book is available from the British Library

ISBN 0 297 82484 8

Designed by Nigel Soper
Edited by Marilyn Inglis
Printed in Italy by Printer Trento srl.

Weidenfeld & Nicolson
Illustrated Division
The Orion Publishing Group
Wellington House
125 Strand
London WC2R 0BB

Picture Credits

Aberglasney Restoration Trust: pages 2–3, 4–5, 12, 14, 15, 19, 26t, 26b, 27t, 27b, 30t, 30b, 48t, 48l, 48r, 49, 50t, 50b, 51, 52, 53t, 54t, 54b, 55t, 56, 57, 62r, 63, 67r, 67b, 69t, 69b, 71t, 71b, 72t, 72l, 72r, 73t, 73m, 73b, 80t, 80l, 82t, 83, 86t, 86l, 87t, 87b, 92l, 92r, 107, 110, 111, 116t, 116b, 131, 132l, 132r, 133, 136t, 139, 144t, 144b, 145t, 146t, 146b, 160t, 160m, 160b, 173, 176, 177. Also pictures on pages 98–101 taken by Michael Dover. Photographs by Kathy de Witt commissioned by Weidenfeld & Nicolson: pages 1, 20, 66, 67l, 80r, 80b, 81, 82b, 84, 85, 86r, 132t, 134t, 134b, 135t, 135b, 136l, 136r, 137t, 137b, 145b, 147, 151, 153, 161, 162. Private Collections: pages 18, 21t, 21b, 31, 122, 139, 140, 128–29, 143, 156, 166l, 166r, 167, 168, 171. By permission of the National Trust: pages 76, 77. National Library of Wales: page 108. By permission of the Carmarthenshire Record Office: pages 125, 126. RCAHM: page 41. British Library: page 17. Mary Evans Picture Library: page 150. Garden plan and section by Michael Ibbotson, from garden designs by Colvin and Moggridge Landscape Architects: pages 178–9.

For further information contact:
The Aberglasney Restoration Trust
Aberglasney, Llangathen
Carmarthenshire SA32 8QH
Telephone and fax: 01558 668998
E-mail: info@aberglasney.org.uk
http://www.aberglasney.org.uk